QUICK TEAM-BUILDING ACTIVITIES FOR BUSY MANAGERS
Second Edition

QUICK
TEAM-BUILDING
ACTIVITIES
FOR
BUSY MANAGERS

50 Exercises That Get Results in Just 15 Minutes

Second Edition

BRIAN COLE MILLER

AMERICAN MANAGEMENT ASSOCIATION
New York I Atlanta I Brussels I Chicago I Mexico City I San Francisco
Shanghai I Tokyo I Toronto I Washington, D. C.

Special discounts on bulk quantities of AMACOM books are available to corporations, professional associations, and other organizations. For details, contact Special Sales Department, AMACOM, a division of American Management Association, 1601 Broadway, New York, NY 10019.
Tel.: 212-903-8316. Fax: 212-903-8083.
Web site: www.amacombooks.org

This publication is designed to provide accurate and authoritative information in regard to the subject matter covered. It is sold with the understanding that the publisher is not engaged in rendering legal, accounting, or other professional service. If legal advice or other expert assistance is required, the services of a competent professional person should be sought.

Library of Congress Cataloging-in-Publication Data
Miller, Brian Cole, 1956–
    Quick team-building activities for busy managers : 50 exercises that get results in just 15 minutes / Brian Cole Miller. — Second edition.
        pages cm
    Revised edition of the author's Quick team-building activities for busy managers, published in 2004.
    Includes bibliographical references and index.
    ISBN 978-0-8144-3633-2 (pbk.) — ISBN 0-8144-3633-1 (pbk.) — ISBN 978-0-8144-3634-9 (ebook) — ISBN 0-8144-3634-X (ebook) 1. Teams in the workplace—Training of. 2. Group relations training. 3. Communication in organizations—Problems, exercises, etc. 4. Interpersonal communication—Problems, exercises, etc. 5. Group games. I. Title.
    HD66.M544 2015
    658.4'022—dc23   2014040872

About AMA
American Management Association (www.amanet.org) is a world leader in talent development, advancing the skills of individuals to drive business success. Our mission is to support the goals of individuals and organizations through a complete range of products and services, including classroom and virtual seminars, webcasts, webinars, podcasts, conferences, corporate and government solutions, business books, and research. AMA's approach to improving performance combines experiential learning—learning through doing—with opportunities for ongoing professional growth at every step of one's career journey.

Printing number

10 9 8 7 6 5 4 3 2 1

CONTENTS

ACKNOWLEDGMENTS

While working with one of my favorite clients in Maine, I ran into two busy managers within minutes of each other. They had similar requests of me. "Brian, can you give me a quick team-building activity? I want to do something to help my staff come together as a team, but we don't have a lot of time. Nothing 'touchy-feely.' Also, nothing that requires any materials or preparation, because I'm late for that staff meeting already!"

From those conversations came the idea for the original book, which has now sold more than 100,000 copies! From Stephen S. Power at AMACOM, came the idea to update this volume by adding more than a dozen exciting new activities, suggestions for how to adapt many activities for use with virtual teams, and improved directions for some activities.

My thanks to the following busy managers and professionals who made time to help me pull both editions together: Bill Weirsma, Wendy Shaw, Dawn Snyder, Gary Siegerst, Brenda Rowe, Alejandro Rodriguez, Eileen Nunley, Dean Miller, Chris Lowe, Leslie Andrews, Lynn Jackson, Mark Hansen, Daina Gold, Kay Doucette, Joe Davy, Rick Damato, Sara Cope, Mylo Cope, Gail Cope, Caroline Cofer, Ed Buns, and Sarah Beaulieu.

The sources of these activities are numerous. I designed many myself. I modified others from existing games and activities. The rest I learned from others in the field, sometimes as I participated at conferences and seminars. I apologize in advance to anyone I may have not credited for their activities.

Thank you Paul Montgomery for the fantastic illustrations.

Biggest thank you to my family—Benjamin, Heidee, Logan, Stacee, Kay, Roger and Theresa, and especially Tim—for their unbridled support and enthusiasm.

INTRODUCTION

This second edition is written for the busy manager who wants to add an element of team-building to a meeting. More than a dozen new activities are included, along with helpful hints for virtual teams. Team-building becomes more difficult when members are in different locations. I've shown how half of the activities in this book can be modified to work with videoconferencing, web meetings, and even simple conference calls. I've also clarified some of the directions for several activities to make them work better with today's technology. You can expect every activity to take less than 15 minutes to conduct and discuss. Busy managers (and their staffs) do not have hours and hours to spend working on their teams. They need activities that are quick and to the point.

Can you really get results in less than 15 minutes? Yes, as long as your expectations are realistic. Longstanding issues will not be resolved. Age-old antagonists will not emerge as best friends. Major obstacles will not disappear. However, important team issues will be brought to light. Strangers will become acquaintances. Group norms will be established. Feelings will be validated. Camaraderie will be enhanced. In the end, a stronger team spirit will be fostered.

All activities can be done with only a few materials, or even none at all. You will not have to run to the store for odd materials to conduct these activities. In fact, more than half of the activities require nothing more than pen and paper! The materials required for the rest of them are simple things often found at work, such as paper clips, markers, index cards, pennies, old magazines, and so forth. Only a few activities require special materials such as a deck of cards, balloons, or a puzzle.

Each activity has one or more specific, focused objective. Teambuilding activities are usually fun, and the ones in this book definitely are. Fun is not the primary focus of any activity in this book, though. Each activity is designed to help your group come together as a team in one way or another. You can have fun while you learn and grow together!

A busy manager like you can run every activity here easily. They are simple to understand and easy to prepare for. Some of them can be conducted successfully moments after you read them for the first time. You can pick up this book on your way to a meeting and use an activity from it right then and there!

The outline for each activity is easy to follow. Each one is presented in the same easy-to-read, bulleted format:

> **This is . . .** explains very briefly what the activity is.

> **The purpose is . . .** tells what the purpose or objective of the activity is.

> **Use this when . . .** gives you clues you should look for that will tell you if this is the right activity for the purpose you and your team are thinking about.

> **Materials you'll need . . .** tells you everything you will need for the activity. Often, it's nothing!

> **Here's how . . .** outlines, step by step, how to conduct the activity.

> **For example . . .** illustrates how the activity may play out, so you get a good sense of what to expect on each one.

> **Ask these questions . . .** lists the best questions for each activity. These are used for the Debrief, the most important part of any team-building activity. During this session, participants discuss

what they learned from the activity and relate it to their behavior back on the job.

Tips for success . . . includes things that will help you run you activity more effectively.

Try these variations . . . offers variations on the activity that can be used to spice it up, slow it down, add a level of competition, or otherwise alter it for a slightly different learning experience.

For virtual teams . . . offers tips for adjusting the activity for groups that meet electronically because the participants cannot be in the same physical location.

Relax, you will not find any of these types of activities here:

NO "fish bowl" activities in which only a few participants are actively involved while everyone else watches and critiques them.

NO role-plays where participants are given a fictitious role to act out or pretend.

NO demonstrations in which the leader makes a point by demonstrating something while all the participants merely watch and then discuss.

NO outdoor activities requiring large areas, nice weather, and physically fit participants.

NO handouts to prepare, copy, or distribute.

NO "touchy-feely" activities in which participants have to touch each other a lot or share intimate thoughts and feelings, activities that push the manager into the role of psychologist rather than activity leader.

Before we get to the activities, two chapters will help you with *any* team-building activity you want to do. The first chapter gives you start-to-finish instructions on how to run an effective team-building activity. We will discuss all three phases of the experience: before, during, and after the activity.

Before the activity, you will learn how to decide which activity is best for you and your team. Why pick *any* activity when you can choose one designed specifically for your team's needs? Then learn how to plan and prepare for your activity (even if you have only 2 minutes in the elevator to do so!).

During the activity, you will learn how to set the activity up for success—giving clear instructions, getting your participants to want to participate, and making sure they know what to do and how to do it. Then learn what you should do while they are engaged. Finally, you will learn how to conduct the most important element of your activity: the Debrief. This is when your participants connect what they did in the activity with their behavior on the job. If you skip this step, you may as well not even have performed the activity!

After the activity, you will learn how to make the things learned during the activity come alive in the workplace and make sure you and your team truly benefit from having done the activity in the first place.

Then, in Chapter 2, we will look at what could go wrong while engaging in an activity. Murphy's law dictates that you will eventually hit a bump or two, but that does not mean you have to fail!

The format for each potential problem is the same:

What if . . . describes the potential problem or concern you may face.

What you'll see . . . indicates what you will actually see and hear that tell you this problem has come up.

The most likely causes . . . identifies what usually causes such a problem. Only when you know the cause can you take meaningful action to avoid the problem altogether or deal with it more effectively.

How to prevent this from ever happening . . . gives ideas on how you can avoid the problem from happening in the first place.

What to do if it happens anyway . . . offers suggestions on how to handle the problem if it actually does happen (despite your best preventive efforts!).

Team-building with your staff can be fun, rewarding, and productive. Seeing those creative sparks as your staff learns something important can be very exciting. Stick with it, be patient, and you will see great results after even just a few activities!

PART ONE

GETTING READY

CHAPTER 1

How to Run a Successful Team-Building Activity

Step 1. Before: Select an activity that's good for your team.

The best team-building *activity* can become the worst team-building *experience* when there is no clear objective. Why spend the time, effort, and money on an activity if you can't identify the business reason or team benefit you expect as a result? If all you want is to have some fun and kill some time, play a parlor game and enjoy. But if you want to improve your team's effectiveness, you need to select an activity that will give you your desired results!

Start with a clear objective in mind. What, specifically, do you want your team to learn or accomplish? Think about it. Your goal should be:

- ➤ Attainable by your team.
- ➤ Relevant and applicable to where the members are as a team right now.
- ➤ Something that will be reinforced long after this activity.

Plan on this activity being one of many small steps your team will start taking now. Remember, an effective team is built primarily on trust. Trust, and thus team-building, can rarely be accomplished in one giant leap.

Match your goal to the activity in this book that will best help you get the results you want. If there is more than one good match, do one activity now and another one at a later date.

A NOTE ON COMPETITION: Competition can be a good thing. It can excite, energize, and challenge people to participate better. Do not assume that competition naturally brings out the best in everyone, though. It can also deflate, discourage, and create unnecessary lingering conflict. As the final judge in competitive activities, you risk becoming "the bad guy" as well. Only you can say how competitive you want your team-building activity to be. The most important thing is to be deliberate in your decision, so you can justify it with a clear objective if necessary. Consider:

- ➤ The current level of competition within the team.
- ➤ The emotional health of the participants in dealing with defeat.
- ➤ How intimidating or intimidated the participants are.
- ➤ Your ability to diffuse real conflict among the team members.

Step 2. Before: Prepare for your team-building activity.

You want to make sure you are ready for everyone to have a great learning experience. Fifteen minutes of planning and preparation ahead of time may not guarantee success, but it will certainly help you prevent disaster. Your activity will be most effective if you go into it feeling competent and confident.

Read through the entire activity several times. Make sure you are clear on what is to happen and when, why, and how. Visualize that activity happening successfully.

Obtain all necessary materials. Check the materials to make sure they will work well for the activity. For example, see that the dates on the pennies are legible, test the markers for any that have dried out, make sure there are no cards missing from the deck, and so forth. Assume nothing! Always have a few extras on hand, just in case.

Practice what you are going to say when you start the activity with your team. The best way to do this is to explain the activity to a friend or colleague. If he or she doesn't understand you, figure out a way to explain things more clearly until he or she does.

If the activity requires you to have a role (card dealer, judge, moderator, etc.), practice your comments or actions. This will help you feel less nervous during the activity. It will also free your mind to focus on more important things (the participants' reactions, the participants' learning, your own observations, etc.) during the activity.

Set up the room. Make sure the tables, chairs, flipcharts, and/or other items are placed so that they contribute to the activity's success. A classroom style row of chairs is usually the least conducive to team-building activities. Better choices include a large circle, a "U" shape, or small table groups (several individuals gathered around each table). Any specific setup information required for an activity is noted within that activity.

If the activity's rules or steps are lengthy, write them ahead of time, and post them on the wall so everyone can see them throughout the activity.

Anticipate potential problems. Visualize the activity with *your* team, in *your* location. Ask yourself what could go wrong. Take action to prevent those problems from occurring and/or plan the corrective actions you can take if they do occur. The most common problems and how to avoid or deal with them are discussed in the next chapter.

Step 3. During: Explain the activity to the team.

A 1-minute introduction can make all the difference in setting your team up for success! People engage better when they know *why* they

are doing something. They also participate better when they understand all the rules up front, and when they are clear on exactly what
is expected of them.

Set the mood. Welcome the team with enthusiasm and optimism.
Team-building is fun! Convey this right away. You don't have to be a
cheerleader; even a smile or a warm comment will let your team know
they are in for a great time.

Explain what the activity is. Give a very brief overview of what you
have planned, so the team can start getting interested and excited.

Explain why you are doing this particular activity. Share with the team
what you hope to accomplish in the next 15 minutes. The more they
see purpose to the activity, the more likely they will participate and
learn what you want them to learn. For a few of the activities in this
book, however, you would ruin their impact by sharing the objective
up front. In those cases, tell them there is an objective that will become
clear to them in a few minutes. Make sure that objective is called out
during the Debrief (the discussion that is held immediately after the
activity).

Explain the activity's rules or steps. Don't be afraid to read from this
book, use notes, or even have them posted on the wall. Speak slowly,
and pause after each one. Remember, they haven't had time to read
and reread the activity like you have. It's usually easier to explain the
activity all at once before responding to any questions from the team.

Have the team move through the activity's steps as you explain them.
For example, if the first step of an activity is to divide the group into
smaller teams, have them actually do that before you tell them the
next step.

A NOTE ON TEAM SIZE: Most activities will not be ruined if smaller groups
are not exactly the same size. If the correct size is critical, the odd

participant or two could be assigned the role of "Observer." The Observer role is to quietly watch the others participate. During the Debrief, the Observer shares his or her unique observations.

A NOTE ON PAIRING UP: When an activity requires the participants to pair up, use your own participation to even things out. Participate if the number is odd; observe if it is even.

Distribute the materials after you've fully explained the activity. Otherwise, you risk people getting distracted by them and missing key points. Distribute the materials before the explanation only if you have found that the materials help people understand things better.

Step 4. During: Check for understanding before beginning.

People often hesitate to ask for help when they are confused. You can clarify misunderstandings with patience and some simple review questions. You can keep competition from getting out of hand by laying down a few ground rules, but they must be agreed upon up front.

Make sure your team understands the activity. Asking *"Do you understand?"* is the least effective way to check this (who wants to answer *"No"* in front of the group?). *"Do you have any questions?"* is a little better. *"What questions do you have?"* is even better.

However, the best way to check their understanding is to ask questions that force the team to review the steps or rules of the activity. For example, *"How many minutes do you have to complete this?"* or *"What happens if one of your balloons pops?"*

When the activity will result in one or more winners, make sure everyone is clear on what criteria will be used to determine who wins. Then, ask a review question such as *"How exactly does someone win?"* If ties need to be broken, explain how that will be done.

Declare up front that you are the final judge on all disagreements about who wins. You don't want the team to argue about who won and lose sight of the real purpose of the activity.

When you are confident everyone understands the activity and is ready to go, ask one last time, *"What remaining questions do you have before we start?"*

Step 5. During: Run the activity.

Letting the team go through the activity, and possibly even fail, may be difficult for you to let happen. Remember, the activity is a low-risk alternative to letting the participants learn from failures on the job! People learn and retain better when they experience lessons, rather than when they just hear them. Sit back, observe, and let your team experience.

Once they begin the activity, see that they are following the steps or rules. You want them to at least get started down the path to success. Hold off on correction for just a moment, though. They may check themselves. If not, gently bring them back to task.

Encourage and support them all. Especially thank anyone who goes first in an activity. Being first is a scary situation for many. It takes courage to go first and risk embarrassment or failure.

Make yourself available to clarify steps or redirect the team. If appropriate, walk around quietly and watch for opportunities to help the team succeed. Be careful not to do their task for them, though.

Throughout the activity, watch for things you will want to bring up later during the Debrief. It is okay to jot down a note or two to remember.

If the activity is timed, watch the clock, and give a "time check" occasionally. For example, *"Time check: you have 2 minutes left."*

Don't stop the activity unless it really runs amok. Otherwise, let it run its course. There will be plenty of opportunity to comment on lessons learned during the Debrief.

Step 6. During: Debrief the activity.

The Debrief is the most critical part of the team-building activity. It is the time when effective questions will guide the participants to link what they experienced in the activity with their behavior on the job. If this step is skipped or glossed over, most of the impact of the activity will be lost in a matter of days. If you do the Debrief well, the lessons learned during the activity will stay with the team indefinitely.

Ask the questions outlined in this book immediately. For most questions, there is no right or wrong answer. Allow all answers to be OK. Try not to evaluate or critique any answer; just nod and accept each one as you listen to it. The questions for each activity should lead the team to the conclusions you want them to reach without you having to spell it out for them.

It is fine to read the questions from this book or to use notes. Stop talking, silently read the question, look back at the team, and then ask the question. The few seconds of silence while you read are less noticeable and less offensive to the group than if you read the question aloud while looking at it. Also, making eye contact while you ask the question is more likely to result in responses than if you do it the other way.

Another way to ask the questions is to write them on index cards beforehand. Pass the index cards out, and ask the participants to take turns reading the questions and soliciting responses.

Try not to call on anyone by name unless you have to. Be comfortable with the silence. Once you have asked a question, stop talking and slowly count to 10 in your head. The silence may feel like an eternity to you, but it feels just as long to the group. Eventually someone will answer! If not, call someone's name before you ask or re-ask a question. This gets their attention so they listen to the question and start formulating a response. They'll feel less put on the spot. Remember, they have never heard your questions before, so it may take a few seconds for them to formulate responses.

Watch for heads nodding, smiles, and other indications that they agree with what is being said by others. Not everyone has to respond to every question for the entire group to learn. If you see reactions that suggest disagreement, ask, *"Does anyone disagree?"* or *"What about an opposing view?"* Call on the one disagreeing only as a last resort.

Repeat or quickly summarize each response offered.

If anyone gives an off-the-wall response or one that is just plain wrong, ask the group how they feel about it rather than correcting someone. This technique will keep it "safe" for all participants to continue answering questions without fear of a reprimand from you.

Even if the activity did not go quite as well as planned, most participants probably learned something. No matter what happened, you can always ask if the group has ever seen anything like this happen back on the job. Ask what can be learned from this experience. The answers may include what can be improved for future team-building activities!

Step 7. After: Reinforce the learning back on the job.

With your help, the activity can continue teaching the participants long after it is over. Reminding participants of the activity and keeping the lessons learned alive will extend its impact. Keep your team focused on behaviors that support the kind of team you are trying to build.

Display anything the team created for the activity back in the workplace. Each time they see that sculpture, flipchart, or cardboard structure, they will be reminded of what they did, how it made them feel, and what it taught them.

If any new terms or special words came up during the activity, use them frequently. Like the visual items mentioned above, these words will prompt a recall of what happened and what they learned.

Refer to the activity and the lessons learned often when you are coaching, giving feedback, or conducting staff meetings. Look for examples of people exhibiting good team behavior related to the activity, and call it out for them and others to see.

If the activity was a huge success, you may want to repeat it soon.

Plan follow-up activities that will reinforce, emphasize, and build upon what was learned this time.

Watch for examples of how the participants used what was learned in the activity and got better results. If you can quantify how their actions are benefiting the organization, call it out for them and others as evidence of success.

Ask participants in your next staff meeting to share what impact the activity has had on them. If you are in remote locations, use e-mail, electronic bulletin boards, and so forth to keep the learning alive.

CHAPTER 2

What Could Go Wrong in a Team-Building Activity

The team-building activities in this book are easy to conduct in most situations. They have been used successfully with hundreds of other groups just like yours. Follow the instructions carefully, and you will be successful, too!

If you have never run such activities before, it is natural to be concerned about what could go wrong. Below are the most common fears and problems managers face in running an activity. Channel the energy your concerns generate into positive actions to avoid problems and/or effectively deal with them if they do happen!

What if . . .   One or more people don't want to participate?

What you'll
see . . .

- ➤ Rolling eyes.
- ➤ Lack of eye contact with you, or other negative body language.
- ➤ Negative comments about the activity or team-building in general.
- ➤ Direct comments that they do not want to participate.
- ➤ Direct refusal to participate.
- ➤ Participants dragging their feet on getting started.

	➤ Suggestions for an alternate activity *("Why don't we just . . .").*
The most likely causes . . .	➤ Past team-building exercises that were unpleasant or unproductive. ➤ Not understanding the purpose or value of the activity. ➤ Shyness or fear of being embarrassed. ➤ The activity doesn't sound fun or worthwhile.
How to prevent this from happening . . .	➤ Be clear about the purpose of the activity when you introduce it to the group. ➤ Be sure the purpose of the activity is one that is needed or valued by the group. ➤ Reassure them that everyone will do it (and no one will be singled out and maybe embarrassed). ➤ If it's an activity that allows this, have the less shy people go first. ➤ If you expect resistance from a particular individual, privately approach him or her beforehand to gain his or her commitment to participate.
What to do if it happens anyway . . .	➤ Unless it's critical, don't make a big deal of it; perhaps after witnessing one or two team-building activities, they will become more willing to participate next time. ➤ Remind them that in order for it to be team-building, everyone must participate; otherwise, the rest of the group won't benefit from the exercise. ➤ Let the group know someone doesn't want to participate, and allow them to handle it. (Beware, they may apply more pressure than you would, or they may not allow that person to participate at all.) ➤ Find a way for the person to still be involved—perhaps as scorekeeper, timekeeper, or observer

(with the expectation that he or she will offer observations after the activity).

What if . . .	They don't understand the directions I am giving?

What you'll see . . .
- Confused looks.
- Participants asking each other what to do.
- Participants not doing what is expected.
- Nothing happens when the activity begins.
- Lots of questions for clarification.

The most likely causes . . .
- Directions were given out of order.
- Directions were poorly explained.
- Sidebar conversations distracted attention.
- Directions were given too fast.
- Directions were too lengthy and not posted.

How to prevent this from even happening . . .
- Read and reread the directions to make sure *you* understand them well.
- Practice explaining the activity to someone before it begins until he or she readily understands it. Use that person's questions to help you adjust the way you explain it during the real thing.
- Pause after each direction to let it sink in.
- Speak slowly as you explain the activity.
- Repeat what seems like the obvious when you give directions (e.g., *"First I want you to pair up. That means we need everyone in groups of two—find one partner to be with right now."*).

What to do if it happens anyway . . .
- Start over. Repeat all the directions, so the difficult ones are put into context. This time, slow down even more.
- Ask someone who did understand to help you explain.

> Do not get frustrated (either with yourself or the team). Stay calm and focused. Be patient with yourself and with them until you are successful.

> Read the directions from the book. If you understood it from the book, they will also.

> If applicable, demonstrate the activity.

What if . . . Materials break, don't work, or we don't have enough?

What you'll see . . .
> Not enough materials to go around.
> Materials breaking or not functioning as planned.

The most likely causes . . .
> Not planning ahead.
> Underestimating the number of materials needed.
> Wrong materials being used.

How to prevent this from even happening . . .
> Bring more than enough materials for all possible participants; err on the side of too many rather than too few.
> Practice or test the activity with exactly the materials you'll be working with (using the exact timeframe) to make sure they will work the way you expect.

What to do if it happens anyway . . .
> Use spare materials (if you have extras).
> Improvise with other materials, if possible.
> Adjust the rules of the activity, if possible.
> Reschedule the activity for another time.

What if . . . Someone gets overly competitive?

What you'll see . . .
> Taking the activity too seriously.
> Bending the rules, or even cheating.
> Extreme efforts to win or do better than others.

	➤ Overly discussing the activity afterward, with a focus on strategies and missed opportunities rather than on learning points.
The most likely causes . . .	➤ A naturally competitive environment in the workplace (e.g., a sales force). ➤ Naturally competitive people. ➤ Conflict in the group. ➤ Too much focus on the activity rather than on learning.
How to prevent this from even happening . . .	➤ Focus the group's attention on the activity's purpose and learning goals when introducing it. ➤ For a naturally competitive group, select activities that encourage teamwork or that have less of an element of competition built into them. ➤ Offer a very minimal prize for the winner during the introduction that will not be a lingering reminder (for example, an exactly 3-second round of applause, rather than a candy bar).
What to do if it happens anyway . . .	➤ Focus the Debrief on what happened, why it happened, group dynamics, and so forth, rather than on who won or did better than whom (you may even have to declare, *"Let's take the focus off the activity itself and discuss what we learned from the activity."*). ➤ Discuss the competitiveness that came out, why it came out, and how helpful or destructive it was. Link those things back to the workplace. ➤ If you must, stop the activity in the middle to remind the group of the activity's purpose and learning goals.
What if . . .	Participants don't join the Debrief discussion?

What you'll see . . .	➤ Lack of eye contact with you, especially right after you ask a question.
	➤ Minimal or one-word responses to your questions.
	➤ Shoulders shrugging.
	➤ Silence.

The most likely causes . . .	➤ They didn't understand your question.
	➤ You haven't given them enough time to formulate an answer.
	➤ They fear embarrassment of a "wrong" answer in front of you or their peers.
	➤ They are angry about something (may be unrelated to the activity).

How to prevent this from even happening . . .	➤ Ask questions slowly.
	➤ Don't be afraid to read the questions from the book.
	➤ Pause (silently count to 10) after each question. This pause may feel like an eternity to you, but it will give participants the time they need to consider an appropriate response.
	➤ Unless they are too far off, accept and appreciate all responses. This is an opportunity to appreciate the diverse thinking styles of your team!
	➤ Minimize the use of closed-ended questions (questions that can be answered easily with a single word, such as yes or no).

What to do if it happens anyway . . .	➤ Reword or restate questions only if the group tells you that they didn't understand the question; otherwise, let them think.
	➤ As a last resort, call on participants by name to respond. Call a name first, then ask the question. This gives participants a chance to focus on the question and prepare a response. They'll feel less put on the spot.
	➤ Explain that the activity is only as valuable as our ability to transfer what we learned from it back to

the workplace. We can start doing that by discussing these questions.

➤ After asking a question, offer your own observation. Then ask what others saw that was similar to or different from what you just shared.

➤ When you get responses, emphatically thank the first few participants for contributing.

➤ If they responded with just a word or two, ask them to clarify, explain, or expound on their answer.

What if . . . Someone dominates the Debrief?

What you'll see . . .
➤ One person answering most of the questions.
➤ One person talking excessively.
➤ Most participants remaining silent.

The most likely causes . . .
➤ The person wanted to help you (and the team) by offering the answers.
➤ The person wanted to show that he or she has the correct answers.
➤ Other participants didn't volunteer answers.
➤ Other participants are afraid to differ with the dominant person.
➤ The person was impatient waiting for others to contribute.
➤ The person doesn't feel like he or she is being heard or taken seriously.
➤ The person may be dominating the group in day-to-day work, and this is just an extension of those group norms.

How to prevent this from even happening . . .
➤ After anyone answers a question, ask, *"What do the rest of you think?"* or *"What else?"* as you make eye contact with other participants. This will give the signal that you are looking for more discussion than just one answer per question.

> Repeat or quickly summarize each comment, and then say, *"Great, who else has an observation?"*

> Be comfortable yourself, waiting for others to respond (a few seconds of silence may encourage others to speak).

> If you expect one person to dominate the discussion, consider talking to that person before the activity and asking him or her to hold back, or encourage others to contribute.

> If the person tends to dominate day to day, begin to address that behavior outside the bounds of this activity.

What to do if it happens anyway . . .

> When asking questions, avoid making eye contact with the dominating individual.

> Begin a few questions with, *"OK, for the rest of you, my next question is . . ."*

> Call on a few participants for their thoughts. Call a name first, then ask the question. This gives participants a chance to focus on the question and prepare a response. They'll feel less put on the spot.

> In an extreme case, ask the person to hold off speaking until others have had a chance to respond.

> Ask, *"Who has a different perspective he or she would like to share with us?"*

What if . . .

The Debrief gets out of hand?

What you'll see . . .

> A gripe session.
> Arguing or fighting.
> Discussion moving off the topic.
> Side bar discussions.

The most likely causes . . .

> Poor questions asked during the Debrief.
> Unresolved team issues.
> Lost control.

How to prevent this from even happening . . .	➤ Unless you are a skilled facilitator, don't veer too far from the questions in this book.
	➤ Do not host activities in hopes of resolving deep issues in the team.
	➤ Ask one or more team members beforehand what kind of reaction they believe the activity will spark in the team. Adjust accordingly.
	➤ Avoid questions that will put anyone on the spot.
	➤ Avoid questions that pit someone against someone else.
What to do if it happens anyway . . .	➤ Step in and stop the discussion(s) before more damage is done; ask, *"How does this discussion apply to what we learned from the activity?"*
	➤ Don't try to assign blame or find the cause.
	➤ Refocus the Debrief with specific, targeted questions (use the questions in this book).
	➤ In a severe case, terminate the activity and Debrief altogether. This may be an ideal time to try to identify the issues at play and figure out what activities to use next.
What if . . .	They don't get what I wanted them to get out of the activity?
What you'll see . . .	➤ Incorrect answers during the Debrief.
	➤ No connection of the activity to the workplace.
	➤ Key participant behaviors or actions during the activity go unnoticed.
The most likely causes . . .	➤ The purpose of the activity was not explained well up front.
	➤ The activity was not the best one to bring out the learning you wanted.
	➤ Debrief questions were not handled well.

How to prevent this from even happening . . .	➤ Be sure to explain the purpose of the activity to the team. Get them to buy into the need to engage and learn.
	➤ Be sure you have a clear learning objective and that the activity you choose will achieve that for your team.
	➤ Be sure your Debrief questions will lead them toward your learning goal without having them feel manipulated.
	➤ Let the participants answer the Debrief questions rather than spoon-feed the correct responses to them.
	➤ When you get minimal responses to Debrief questions, ask for clarification or elaboration.
	➤ Avoid helping the participants get through the activity. The more you help, the less they experience, and thus the less they learn and grow.
What to do if it happens anyway . . .	➤ Disclose to the group what lesson you had hoped to teach, and discuss where that lesson was found in the activity.
	➤ Let it go; accept what they did learn, and build upon that.
	➤ If time permits, redo the activity with a renewed focus on the desired objective.
	➤ Be open to new or different learning than you had expected or wanted. Perhaps the "aha" moments that the group experiences are just the "aha" moments they truly need at this time

A FINAL NOTE: Remember, your participants want their activity to be successful just as much as you do!

PART TWO

THE ACTIVITIES

CHAPTER 3

Communication: Listening and Influencing

CARD TRIANGLES

This is . . .	A negotiation activity in which teams trade pieces of playing cards in hopes of finding complete cards.
The purpose is . . .	Participants learn to see others' perspectives before they can influence and persuade.
Use this when . . .	➤ Individuals are focusing too much on their own needs.
	➤ Individuals need to hone their sales skills.
	➤ Individuals need to develop their negotiation skills.
Materials you'll need . . .	➤ A deck of playing cards.
	➤ Cut each card in half diagonally, then in half diagonally again, so each card is now in four triangle quarters.
	➤ Mix all the pieces well, and place an equal number of pieces in the same number of envelopes as you will have teams.
	➤ Small prizes for the winners (optional).
Here's how . . .	1. Divide the group into teams of three or four.
	2. Give each team an envelope containing playing card triangles.
	3. The teams have 3 minutes to examine and sort their pieces and plan their strategy for bartering.
	4. Open the bartering. Everyone participates by bartering for the pieces their team needs. (They may barter individually or as a team.)

5. Allow 8 minutes for bartering.

6. Count the teams' completed cards, and announce the winning team.

Ask these questions . . .

➤ How willing were others to trade with you?

➤ What negotiation tactics were most successful for you? *(Seeing what they wanted and offering that; Being aggressive; Being a nice guy, etc.)*

➤ How did your strategy change during play? Why?

➤ What other skills did you have to draw on to be successful? *(Listening; empathy; giving a personal touch; creative problem solving; etc.)*

➤ In what work situations do we find ourselves negotiating for time, information, or resources?

➤ What implication does this have for us back on the job?

Tips for success . . .

➤ You must have at least three teams for this activity to work well. If your group is small, each team should consist of two participants.

➤ They can barter individually or as teams.

➤ Give a 2-minute warning before play is to end.

➤ Observe whether two or more teams combine might. Comment during the Debrief.

Try these variations . . .

➤ For smaller groups, give each participant an envelope, and have them all barter individually rather than in teams.

➤ For smaller groups, use only half of the deck of cards.

➤ After 4 minutes of play, give the teams 2 minutes to form coalitions. Any two teams that want to merge may do so before resuming play. Make sure there was an even number of teams to begin with. What influenced your team's decision to merge? And with whom?

> For a simpler and quicker activity, cut the cards only in half, not in fourths.

For virtual teams . . . This activity is not suitable for virtual teams.

COPY CAT

This is . . . An activity in which participants make an exact copy of a "scultpure."

The purpose is . . . Participants learn the importance of listening, as well as of clear communications.

Use this when . . .
- ➤ Individuals are focusing too much on their own way of doing things.
- ➤ The group needs to practice listening.
- ➤ Individuals are not being clear and concise in their communications.

Materials you'll need . . .
- ➤ A set of six to seven common office items for each participant (see note below).
- ➤ A visual barrier to place between each pair of participants—a file folder or a large binder works well.
- ➤ A stopwatch or a phone with a stopwatch feature.

Here's how . . .
1. Have the participants pair up.
2. Distribute a set of identical office items to each partner.
3. Have each pair set up a visual barrier between themselves. It's okay if they can the items belonging to other team members, but not their partner's.
4. Instruct one partner (the Architect) of each pair to build some kind of structure using only the items provided. This should take about 1 minute.

5. Explain that their partners (the Builders) will try to copy the structure on their side of the barrier.
6. When you give the signal, the Builders have 2 minutes to finish (set your stopwatch).
7. Both partners may talk freely, but they may not ask any questions of each other.
8. Builders may not peek at the Architect's structure, nor may Architects peek at their Builder's progress.
9. After time is up, remove barriers and view results.
10. Reverse roles and repeat the activity from Step 3. This time, allow questions.

For example . . .

Common office items to include in the set may include: A paper cup, a flipchart marker, a business card, a paperback book, a paper clip, a sticky note pad, a packet of sugar, an item that is organizationally specific, a plastic fork, a thumbtack, etc.

Ask these questions . . .

➤ What strategies did you use during the activity? *(I explained it very slowly; I listened very carefully.)*
➤ Which were most helpful?
➤ In which round were your sculptures closest to each other? Why?
➤ How did you feel when questions weren't allowed; when they were allowed? *(frustrated; like one hand was tied behind my back; liberated; like I still wanted to peek; more natural communications; etc.)*
➤ How intently did you have to listen and pay attention? Is that the same kind of attention you give others in meetings or on the phone? Why or why not?
➤ What implications does this have for us back on the job?

Tips for success . . .	➤ You may use many different items, just as long as each pair of participants has identical sets of items. So, one pair may each have a cup, paper clip, book, marker, coin, and computer mouse, while another pair may have a cup, paper clip, sticky note pad, marker, coin, and water bottle.
	➤ Don't help or direct the Architects. What they create is irrelevant to the activity's learning goals.
Try these variations . . .	➤ Save time by doing just one round before your Debrief.
	➤ Use a set of children's wood blooks of different shapes or sizes. This will make the activity more difficult because the participants now have to create a vocabulary (names for the different blocks: the wedge, the box, etc.) on top of everything else.
	➤ Use a set of children's wooden alphabet blocks. You will likely not be able to make identical sets (even the letters!) for each participant, so declare up front that the letters on the blocks may be ignored.
	➤ Conduct a mini Debrief after the first round, then a fuller Debrief after the second round.
	➤ Allow questions throughout both rounds. Direct the Debrief to focus more on listening skills. How many of you Builders found yourselves thinking of other things? Why do you think that was the case for this silly activity? When you're listening to each other in a meeting (or to customers), do you let your mind wander?
For virtual teams . . .	This activity works well for virtual teams.
	1. Step 2 may have to happen in advance. Either send a set of identical materials to each pair or have each pair retrieve an identical set of items locally.

2. Then follow Steps 4 to 10.
3. At Step 9, have pairs turn their webcam to show results to each other or take a picture to send to their partners.

LISTEN UP

This is . . .	A speaking activity in which participants listen as others share their views on a controversial topic.
The purpose is . . .	Participants practice listening skills even when they are anxious to agree emphatically or strongly challenge.
Use this when . . .	➤ Individuals are not listening carefully. ➤ Individuals feel like others are not listening with open minds. ➤ Individuals want to get to know each other better.
Materials you'll need . . .	➤ An identical set of 10 to 15 index cards for each team. On each card in the set, you will have written a different controversial topic.
Here's how . . .	1. Have the participants pair up. 2. Give each pair a set of prepared index cards. 3. One partner draws a card and speaks for 3 minutes nonstop about her views on the topic. 4. Her partner may not say anything, just listen. 5. After 3 minutes, her partner has 1 minute to recap what he heard. This is not the time to rebut, debate, or agree—just summarize. 6. Reverse roles, and repeat with a new topic.
For example . . .	Controversial topics may include same-sex marriage, abortion, prayer in schools, euthanasia, election finance reform, capital punishment, income tax reform, needle exchange for drug users, unions, social security

reform, reform, immigration, gun control, funding for the space program, AIDS, nuclear arms, and so forth.

Ask these questions . . .

- ➤ How did the speakers' tone and body language contribute to the message?
- ➤ How did you feel listening without being able to speak your mind? *(Frustrated; anxious; made me listen better; etc.)*
- ➤ How did you feel speaking without your listener saying anything? *(Like I was being heard; frustrated that I did not know where she was on the issue; etc.)*
- ➤ How was the listener's summary?
- ➤ When is it especially important for us to listen this attentively at work?
- ➤ What implication does this have for us back on the job?

Tips for success . . .

- ➤ Participants can reject up a topic if they are uncomfortable discussing it.
- ➤ You can use one large set of index cards for the whole group. Duplicate cards are fine. Have enough cards for each participant (and a few extras). Distribute one card to each team. After one person has talked, distribute another card to the other participant. Do not give both participants their cards at the beginning of the activity. The second participant will be tempted to focus on what he plans to say when he should be listening to his partner!
- ➤ Give a 30-second warning before play is to end.

Try these variations . . .

- ➤ Choose the controversial topics so that they are all related to your industry, field, or organization.
- ➤ After the first participant speaks on a topic for 3 minutes, allow the second participant to speak

on the same topic for 3 minutes. Discuss how two monologues are different from one discussion.

➤ Allow the listener to speak, but only to ask questions to understand better the other person's position.

For virtual teams . . .

This activity works for virtual teams.

1. After Step 1, publish a list of controversial topics and allow participants to select one.
2. Then participants follow Steps 3 to 6 via phone or chat functions.

ME, MYSELF, AND I

This is . . .   A story-telling activity that forces participants to communicate about anything except themselves.

The purpose is . . .   Participants see how often their communication is centered on themselves.

Use this when . . .
- Individuals need to improve their communication skills to focus less on themselves and more on others.
- Individuals need to focus on listening skills.
- Individuals need to practice creativity (around communication techniques).
- You don't have prep time and/or materials for anything more elaborate.

Materials you'll need . . .
- No materials are necessary for this activity.

Here's how . . .
1. Have the participants pair up.
2. One partner begins by speaking for 3 minutes nonstop. He must continue talking without any pauses.
3. He may speak about any topic or several topics.
4. He may never use the word "I."
5. The listening partner may not speak at all, not even to ask questions or say "uh-huh."
6. After 3 minutes, reverse roles, and repeat.

Ask these questions . . .	➤ Which role was easier for you, the speaker or the listener? Why?
	➤ How did you feel listening without being able to ask questions or contribute your own thoughts? *(Left out; less connected; more focused on the speaker; etc.)*
	➤ How did you feel speaking without being able to check in with your listener? *(Worried that he was not understanding or did not care; uncomfortable with the attention on me; enjoying the attention and focus; etc.)*
	➤ How difficult or easy was it to keep talking non-stop? Why?
	➤ What creative ways did you find to talk about yourself without using "I?"
	➤ How can we phrase our communications to focus better on the other person?
	➤ What implications does this have for us back on the job?
Tips for success . . .	➤ Be prepared to demonstrate a portion of a 2-minute monologue without using "I." Have the group try to catch you using an "I."
	➤ Give a 30-second warning before the play ends.
Try these variations . . .	➤ Add a get-to-know-you element by having participants determine who is the first speaker and listener by who is oldest, who lives furthest from your location, who has the next birthday, or the cutest pet, who is most physically fit, and so forth.
	➤ Extend the speaking time to 5 minutes to make it more difficult.
	➤ Add competitiveness by allowing the listeners to earn two points each time the speaker says "I" and one point when the speaker pauses for more than 5 seconds. Be prepared with small prizes for the

winner(s). During the Debrief, ask how the competitiveness impacted the activity.

For virtual   Each variation listed can work well for a virtual team.
teams . . .   If audio is not available, participants may key in their comments.

NAPKINS

This is . . .   A activity in which participants demonstrate creative and different uses for a common napkin.

The purpose is . . .   Participants practice thinking creatively and learn to listen and value the opinions and perspectives of others.

Use this when . . .
> Individuals need to hone their influencing skills.
> Creative problem solving is not happening very much.
> Individuals are not cooperating well with others.

Materials you'll need . . .
> One large cloth napkin for each team.

Here's how . . .
1. Divide the group into teams of three to five participants.
2. Give each team a napkin and 5 minutes to prepare its demonstration.
3. Each team presents an original use for the napkin.
4. While demonstrating their idea, participants may not speak.

Ask these questions . . .
> How did your team arrive at its original use for the napkin?
> How did you process each other's ideas? (*We just went around the circle and voted; we used "thumbs-up"*

voting as the idea was being shared; we just went with the first idea because it was so good; etc.)

➤ Who did the most listening? The best listening? And, who did the most talking?

➤ What assumptions did you operate under? (*That it had to do with dining; that we must appeal to consumers rather than businesses; that we couldn't add anything to the design; etc.*)

➤ How did your assumptions limit or expand your creativity?

➤ How did not being able to speak affect the way you presented the original use for your napkin?

➤ What implications does this have for us back on the job?

Tips for success . . .

➤ Have one or two offbeat ideas yourself before the activity begins. If the teams get really stuck, demonstrate your ideas to get their creative juices flowing. ONLY do this if necessary (otherwise you run the risk of their clinging to your ideas instead of creating their own).

➤ Refrain from commenting on their creative process. Even positive comments ("I like where this is going") can get in the way of the creative process.

➤ Announce at the beginning of the activity if they are allowed to use anything else with the napkin (keys, a pen, paper, water, etc.).

Try these variations . . .

➤ Introduce a level of competition by having teams vote for the best original use of the napkin.

➤ Use an item different from a napkin, but equally simple (cardboard box, large garbage bag, etc.).

➤ Give each team a pair of scissors and allow the members to cut the napkin if they want. Or, one safety pin. Or some other item that they may (or must?) use in their original design.

> ➤ Rather than a demonstration, have the teams present a 30-second commercial for the napkin based on their original use for it.

For virtual teams . . .   This activity is not suitable for virtual teams.

ORIGAMI

This is . . .	An activity in which participants follow instructions to fold a sheet of paper while keeping their eyes closed.
The purpose is . . .	Participants see how instructions can be interpreted differently and, thus, how clear our communications need to be.
Use this when . . .	➤ Individuals are not communicating clearly or specifically. ➤ Individuals make too many assumptions about their listeners. ➤ You don't have prep time and/or materials for anything more elaborate.
Materials you'll need . . .	➤ One sheet of paper for each participant.
Here's how . . .	1. Give each participant a sheet of paper. 2. Announce that you will give them instructions on how to fold their paper. 3. Have them close their eyes and keep them closed. They may not ask questions while you are delivering your instructions. 4. Give instructions to fold and rip their papers several times. 5. Have everyone open their eyes, unfold their papers, and compare what the results.

For example . . .	➤ Fold your paper in half.
	➤ Now, fold it in half again.
	➤ Then, fold it in half one more time.
	➤ Now, rip off the right corner.
	➤ Turn your paper over and rip off the upper corner.
Ask these questions . . .	➤ Did everyone come up with the same end result? Why or why not?
	➤ How would the results have been different if your eyes were open? *(We could have compared and copied what others were doing; etc.)*
	➤ How did you feel as I was giving the instructions? *(Confused; I wanted to ask questions; frustrated with you; etc.)*
	➤ How could my instructions have been improved?
	➤ What implication does this have for us back on the job?
Tips for success . . .	➤ Give the instructions slowly and deliberately. You are not trying to lose them or trick them. Repeat as necessary.
	➤ Do not correct anyone as he or she is folding. There is no one right answer. The instructions are deliberately ambiguous.
	➤ Watch to see if anyone opens his or her eyes. When is it appropriate to break the rules?
Try these variations . . .	➤ Invite participants to give the directions to the group. See if they can accomplish more consistent results after your Debrief.
	➤ Allow the participants to keep their eyes open, but make the folding more complex.
	➤ Use origami paper, and give the instructions for folding it into an origami shape.

For virtual teams . . . This activity works well for virtual teams.

1. Follow Steps 1 to 4, ensure that all participants' papers are the same size and shape.
2. At Step 5, participants show their origami on webcam, or they send or post a picture of it.
3. Each variation of this activity can work for a virtual team.

SHARED VALUES

This is . . .   A sharing activity in which participants come to agreement on the most important shared values to the group.

The purpose is . . .   Participants come to agreement on the most important values they share.

Use this when . . .
- ➤ A significant project or work effort is beginning.
- ➤ Individuals feel like others are not listening with open minds.
- ➤ Individuals need to bond together.

Materials you'll need . . .
- ➤ Paper and a pen for each participant.
- ➤ One piece of flipchart paper for each team.
- ➤ Colored markers.

Here's how . . .
1. Have each participant take 2 minutes to write down what he or she feels are the three most important values to your organization.
2. Divide the group into teams of four to six participants.
3. Have each participant share three values with the team.
4. From all the values shared, the team must agree on the three most important for your organization.
5. Give each team a piece of flipchart paper and some colored markers.

6. Each team creates a poster with words, symbols, and/or pictures that reflects those three values.

7. After 10 minutes, have each team present their poster to the group.

For example . . . Values include commitment to customers, integrity, teamwork, leadership, quality focus, innovation, efficiency, respect, creativity, learning, and so forth.

Ask these questions . . .
- ➤ What values seem to be common across teams?
- ➤ How did you handle disagreements in the teams?
- ➤ If someone new to the organization saw these lists of values, how do you think they would expect people to behave?
- ➤ Do we behave like that?
- ➤ What can cause us to lose sight of our values? *(Pressing deadlines; others acting differently; changes at work; etc.)* What can we do when that happens?
- ➤ How would living these values help us meet our goals?
- ➤ What implication does this have for us back on the job?

Tips for success . . .
- ➤ Encourage the teams to be creative in their representation of the values.
- ➤ If your organization already has stated values, have the teams still try to identify the three most important for this part of the organization.
- ➤ If a team does not finish, ask what prevented them from doing so. Others will learn from their difficulties. Then ask how those barriers could have been avoided or dealt with effectively.
- ➤ At Step 4, announce that their agreed values must not contain "and," as that would be an easy way to include more than three. The conversation to

prioritize and eliminate is almost as important as the result.

➤ In the coming days, periodically ask which values are being demonstrated on the job.

Try these variations . . .
➤ If your organization (or just your department) does not have a mission statement, have the teams make a poster to present what your mission statement should be. Remember, a mission statement explains why the organization exists, not its goals.

➤ If your organization (or just your department) does not have a vision statement, have the teams make a poster to present what your vision should be. Remember, the vision statement tells where you hope to be in the future.

For virtual teams . . .
This activity works well for virtual teams.

1. After Steps 1 and 2, participants convene via conference call, cell phones, instant messaging, etc., to complete Steps 3 and 4.
2. At Step 5, team members prepare a minipresentation to the rest of the team using whatever technology and resources are available.
3. Each variation listed can work for a virtual team.

CHAPTER 4

Connecting: Getting to Know Each Other

GOSSIP TIME

This is . . . An activity in which participants share fun or complimentary gossip about each other and then try to guess who said what.

The purpose is . . . Participants learn new and interesting things about each other. This may prompt further appreciation for each other and stronger personal ties.

Use this when . . .
- ➤ Individuals know each other quite well.
- ➤ There is a comfortable trust among the group.
- ➤ You don't have prep time and/or materials for anything more elaborate.

Materials you'll need . . .
- ➤ Paper and pencils or pens for each participant.

Here's how . . .
1. One person volunteers (or is volunteered!) to be the first Target.
2. Everyone else writes one thing about the Target on a slip of paper. It can be complimentary or a bit surprising.
3. Collect the statements, and randomly select one to read aloud.
4. The Target gets one chance to guess who wrote it.
5. If the Target guesses incorrectly, read the next statement. Each time a statement is read, the Target has one chance to guess its author.

6. Play continues until the Target can correctly identify the source of a particular statement. Then read the rest of the notes aloud.

7. The auther of the paper that the Target correctly identified becomes the next Target, and another round begins from Step 2.

8. Play as many rounds as time allows or until energy for the activity wanes.

For example . . .
"Someone says you are still in love with Ringo Starr!"
"Someone called you a good listener."
"Someone says you sing great karaoke."

Ask these questions . . .
➤ How much did you learn about each other?
➤ How embarrassed (or proud) were you when you were the Target?
➤ What made it difficult (or easy) for you to guess who authored the comments?

Tips for success . . .
➤ Keep the mood light and fun. Protect the group from mean or inappropriate remarks.
➤ Don't let the Target read the papers. He or she may be able to identify the source by the handwriting.
➤ You may ask the Target to leave the room while the others write, so that he or she cannot see who doesn't turn in a paper.
➤ If time is limited, you don't have to wait for every person to write something.

Try these variations . . .
➤ Limit the comments to only work-related or even project-related items.
➤ If you limit the comments to only complimentary items, this becomes a Recognition activity.
➤ You can focus this activity on a particular learning goal. Limit the comments to the Target's

communication style, interpersonal relationships, teamwork, and problem-solving abilities or techniques or other work-related goals.

For virtual teams . . .

This activity works well for virtual teams.

1. Complete Step 2 in advance. Have participants write one statement about each of the other participants.
2. Use only one set of statements about one participant (Target) at a time.
3. A variation: Don't do Step 2 in advance. After Step 1, the Target doesn't look at the screen while you randomly read the statements that other participants have submitted.
4. Another variation: Don't do Step 2 in advance. Have each participant text, instant message, or email their statement directly to you. Randomly read them aloud until the Target guesses correctly.
5. Each variations listed can work for a virtual team.

HUMAN BILLBOARDS

This is . . .	A self-disclosure activity in which participants create a poster about themselves.
The purpose is . . .	Participants learn more about each other and connect on a personal level.
Use this when . . .	➤ Individuals do not know each other very well. ➤ One or more of the individuals are new to the team. ➤ A new team is forming.
Materials you'll need . . .	➤ One flipchart paper for each participant. ➤ Colored markers. ➤ Scissors.
Here's how . . .	1. Give each participant a piece of flipchart paper and some colored markers. 2. Each participant has 6 minutes to use words, pictures, or symbols to describe themselves on the "billboard." 3. Cut a slit or an "X" near the top of the paper so each participant can fit his or her head through it. 4. Participants put their billboard on so it drapes in front of them. 5. Encourage them to mingle for 6 minutes.

6. While mingling, they can only ask questions about another's billboard or respond to questions asked of them.

Ask these questions . . .
> Why is it important for us to know each other outside of a purely work-related context?
> How difficult (or easy) was it to share information about yourself with others?
> How can we learn more about each other back on the job?

Tips for success . . .
> Reassure those who are reluctant and those who do not know what to write that they only need to share what they are comfortable disclosing now.
> Have them print their names on their billboards and post them around the break room, conference room, or lunchroom so they can refer to them and continue to reach out to others.
> You may use this activity just to get acquainted or get a meeting started without asking the Debrief questions afterward.
> You can use this activity more than once with the same group. Use one of the variations below.

Try these variations . . .
> Direct what will go on the billboard. It can be centered on one theme, such as career; company/organization; nonwork; favorites (e.g., color, food, book, movie, U.S. President); wishes and dreams; and so forth.
> Instead of a billboard, have participants create a screen saver, T-shirt, bumper sticker, personal flag, license plate, tattoo, and so forth.
> You may use regular 8½″ × 11″ paper instead of flipchart paper and have participants tape them to their chests.

> ➤ You may use tape and string to make a neck holder for the billboard, rather than cutting it.

For virtual   This activity is not suitable for virtual teams.
teams . . .

MY N.A.M.E.

This is . . . An activity in which participants introduce themselves by presenting their first names as acronyms.

The purpose is . . . Everyone knows everyone else's name and some interesting things about each other. That information may prompt some small talk later.

Use this when . . .
➤ One or more of the individuals' names are not known.
➤ Individuals do not know each other very well.
➤ You don't have prep time and/or materials for anything more elaborate.

Materials you'll need . . .
➤ No materials are necessary for this activity.

Here's how . . .
1. Give group members 3 to 5 minutes to think of interesting facts about themselves that correspond to the letters of their first name.
2. Have each participant share his or her acronym.

For example . . . "Hi, I'm Logan. L is for Led Zepplin, one of my favorite rock groups. O is for Ohio, which is where I live. G is for German, the only foreign language I know. A is for Aunt Wendee, my favorite relative. And N is for Nice, because I am a nice guy!"

Ask these questions . . .
➤ Why is it important for us to know each other beyond a purely work-related context?

> How difficult (or easy) was it to share information about yourself with others?

> How can we learn more about each other back on the job?

Tips for success . . .

> If participants get stuck, tell them they do not have to follow the rules strictly. For example, "L" can be for Loving chocolate, Loving chess, Loving snow, and so forth.

> Be prepared to share your own acronym as an example for the group.

> You may use this activity just to get acquainted or get a meeting started without asking the Debrief questions afterward.

Try these variations . . .

> Instead of acronyms about themselves, have the participants create acronyms from their first names that correspond to the kind of work they do (customer service, research, etc.), a current project they are working on, or a problem they collectively face (you may be surprised at a few creative ideas for resolution!).

For virtual teams . . .

Each variation listed can work well for a virtual team. If audio is not available, participants may key in their comments.

NEIGHBORS

This is . . .   An activity in which participants learn each other's names.

The purpose is . . .   Participants of new teams learn each other's names and maybe some interesting things about each other.

Use this when . . .
- ➤ Individuals do not know each other at all.
- ➤ A large team is coming together for the first time.
- ➤ Variations of this activity (see below) are good for teams whose members know each other's names, but not much else about one another.
- ➤ You don't have prep time and/or materials for anything more elaborate.

Materials you'll need . . .
- ➤ No materials are necessary for this activity.

Here's how . . .
1. Have the participants stand in a circle with one person in the middle.
2. Give everyone a moment to memorize the first, middle, and last names of of their neighbors—the person to their left and to their right.
3. The person in the middle of the circle points to someone and says either "left neighbor" or "right neighbor."
4. That participant must say the full name of his or her neighbor. If he or she pauses or stumbles on

the name, that person trades places with the person in the middle.

5. Play continues until it seems that everyone knows each others' names. When that happens, call out "New Neighbors!," and everyone must move to a new space.

6. Repeat Steps 2 to 5.

Ask these questions . . .
- ➤ Why is it important to know each other's names when we begin a team?
- ➤ Other than to make the game a bit more challenging, why would we want to know each other's middle names?
- ➤ What else did you learn about your teammates during this activity?

Tips for success . . .
- ➤ Insist on middle names (to make the game challenging enough to hold their interest).
- ➤ Allow them a moment to learn each other's names. Perhaps encourage them to share the story (if there is one) behind their middle name or why they go by their middle instead of first name.
- ➤ It's better to call "New Neighbors" sooner rather than later. It's okay if not everyone has been tested on the names of both their neighbors. The point is for them to remember those names, not have to prove it.

Try these variations . . .
- ➤ If the team members know each other's names, have them learn their neighbors' hometowns, favorite sports team, or some other interesting fact(s).
- ➤ For smaller teams, play with names, then use the variation above so teams start to learn more about each other.

➤ At Step 2, have participants also learn one interesting fact about their neighbors. At Step 3, the person in the middle doesn't announce "left neighbor" or "right neighbor," but merely points at a participant. Then at Step 4, that participant's neighbors must announce to the group that participant's name and the interesting fact about him or her.

For virtual teams . . .   This activity is not suitable for virtual teams.

A PENNY FOR YOUR THOUGHTS

This is . . .   A light introduction activity that reveals a quick, personal fact about each participant.

The purpose is . . .   Everyone knows everyone else's name and one interesting fact about each other. That information may prompt some small talk later.

Use this when . . .
- One or more of the individual's names are not known.
- Individuals do not know each other very well.
- You don't have prep time and/or materials for anything more elaborate.

Materials you'll need . . .
- One penny for each participant. The best pennies are shiny, easy to read, and less than 20 years old.

Here's how . . .
1. Give a penny to each participant. (As you're doing this, jokingly ask if they realized that they were going to receive a "cash bonus" for attending today!).
2. First ask them to introduce themselves with their name and any other information you want shared with the group.
3. Then ask them to share something significant or interesting about themselves from the year on their penny.
4. You go first to set the example.

For example . . .	"Hi, I'm Ruth. I've been at this company 14 years and in this department for 3 years. My penny says 1999, and that's the year I let my husband talk me into going skydiving with him!"
Ask these questions . . .	➤ Why is it important for us to know more about each other? ➤ How difficult (or easy) was it to share information about yourself with others? ➤ How can we learn more about each other back on the job?
Tips for success . . .	➤ Give them a moment to think of something to say before beginning. ➤ When you want them to share more than two pieces of information besides their name, list what you want on a chart or board. ➤ If someone says she can't remember anything significant from that year, encourage her to describe what was going on in her life at that time (where she was living, what job she had, hobbies she was pursuing, etc.), or use one of the variations listed below, or give her a different penny. ➤ This activity can be used with the same group more than once (since participants are unlikely to get a penny with the same year a second time). ➤ If you don't have pennies, participants can just pull coins out of their own pockets or purses. ➤ You may use this activity just to get acquainted or get a meeting started without asking the Debrief questions afterward.
Try these variations . . .	➤ Have participants explain what would be different if they could relive that year, or how their lives would be different if that year never happened.

- ➤ Have participants tell their favorite song, movie, TV show, or other entertainment from that year.
- ➤ Don't use pennies; just have participants identify the best year of their life and explain why it was so outstanding.
- ➤ If you have time, let the group ask questions after each participant shares her information *(Had your husband been skydiving before?; Where did you dive?; Have you done it since?; Would you even want to?; etc.).*

For virtual teams . . .

This activity works well for virtual teams.

1. At Step 1, tell participants in advance to have a penny with them.
2. Then follow Steps 2 to 4.
3. Each variation listed can work for a virtual team.

 **? RATHER THAN**

This is . . .	A light introductory activity that reveals each participant's personal preferences.
The purpose is . . .	Everyone knows one personal preference about each other. That information may then prompt some small talk later.
Use this when . . .	➤ One or more of the individuals are new to the team. ➤ Individuals do not know each other very well. ➤ You don't have prep time and/or materials for anything more elaborate.
Materials you'll need . . .	➤ No materials are necessary for this activity.
Here's how . . .	1. Sit in a circle so everyone can see each other if possible. 2. Start by declaring something that you like to do. 3. The participant next to you restates what you said and then says something that he would *rather* do than that. 4. The next participant restates what was just said and then says something that *she* would rather do than that. 5. Continue around the room.
For example . . .	"I like to collect porcelain dolls." "Rather than collect porcelain dolls, I like to eat ice cream."

"Rather than eat ice cream, I like to sunbathe on the beach."
"Rather than sunbathe on the beach, I like to surf the Net."
"Rather than surf the Net, I like to coach my daughter's soccer team."

Ask these questions . . .
- ➤ Why is it important for us to know each other beyond a purely work-related context?
- ➤ How difficult (or easy) was it to share information about yourself with others?
- ➤ How can we learn more about each other back on the job?

Tips for success . . .
- ➤ Play can go around the room indefinitely.
- ➤ Allow the group to react briefly to comments but not to dwell on anyone's statement (and certainly not to criticize)—however bizarre or unpopular!
- ➤ You may use this activity just to get acquainted or get a meeting started without asking the Debrief questions afterward.

Try these variations . . .
- ➤ Specify a category (such as your team and its work, your company/organization, non-work-related activities, information related to hobbies, etc.).
- ➤ Make this an ice breaker/introductory activity by merely asking the participants to preface their "Rather Than" comment with their name. For example, "My name is Derek, and rather than eat ice cream. . . ."
- ➤ Play "Worse Than." Declare something you don't like. The next participant declares something that would be worse for him. For example, "Worse than going to the dentist would be getting lost in a new city."

For virtual
teams . . .

This activity works well for virtual teams.

1. At Step 1, establish a virtual circle—put the participants in an order they can follow in Steps 3 and 4.
2. Then follow Steps 2 to 5.
3. Each variation listed can work for a virtual team.

READY, SET, REORGANIZE!

This is . . .   An activity in which participants organize themselves based on various pieces of information about themselves.

The purpose is . . .   Participants learn new and interesting facts about each other. That information may then prompt some small talk later.

Use this when . . .
- ➤ One or more of the individuals are new to the team.
- ➤ Individuals do not know each other very well.
- ➤ You don't have prep time and/or materials for anything more elaborate.

Materials you'll need . . .
- ➤ No materials are necessary for this activity.

Here's how . . .
1. Divide the group in half. Stand participants in lines facing each other.
2. Announce a category (for example, first name).
3. Both teams reorganize themselves alphabetically by first name as quickly as possible.
4. Announce another category (for example, home address street name).
5. Both teams reorganize themselves in this new alphabetical order as quickly as possible.
6. Repeat for as many categories as you want.

For example . . .	Additional sorting categories could be last name, birthday (chronologically), favorite food (from spiciest to blandest), pet's name, length of time at current organization (numerically), birthplace (alphabetically or geographically from east to west), fantasy vacation destination, formal job title, number of U.S. states visited in their lifetime (numerically), and so forth.
Ask these questions . . .	➤ Why is it important for us to know each other beyond a purely work-related context? ➤ How difficult (or easy) was it to share information about yourself with others? ➤ What surprises did you have when reorganizing yourselves? ➤ How can we learn more about each other back on the job?
Tips for success . . .	➤ Think of more categories than you will need. It is better to have too many than not enough. ➤ Stop the game when the energy or enthusiasm starts to fade. ➤ This game can be played again with different categories or when a new member joins the team. ➤ You may use this activity just to get acquainted or get a meeting started without asking the Debrief questions afterward.
Try these variations . . .	➤ If the group is large (more than 18 participants), divide into three competing teams. ➤ Give small prizes for the team that is fastest. ➤ Halfway through the game, the teams combine into one line for a category. Once they have sorted themselves, divide them in half at the midpoint of the long line. They now are two new teams.

Continue the game, and the participants will get to know the new players on their team.

➤ Keep the participants in one group for all sorting.
➤ If the enthusiasm is high, ask the group to come up with a new category.

For virtual teams . . .   This activity is not suitable for virtual teams.

SIMILARITIES AND DIFFERENCES

This is . . .   An introductory activity in which participants are challenged to learn how they are similar and different from each other.

The purpose is . . .   Participants learn new and interesting things about each other and connect with each other on a personal level.

Use this when . . .
- Individuals do not know each other very well.
- A significant project or work effort is beginning.
- Individuals do not appreciate each other very much.

Materials you'll need . . .
- An index card (or sheet of paper) and a pen for each participant.

Here's how . . .
1. Give each participant an index card and a pen.
2. Have them divide their cards into three columns with the headings: "Name, Similar, and Different."
3. Have them mingle and try to fill their card with as many names as possible.
4. For each name, they find something that they have in common with the other person and one way in which they are different.

For example . . .	Name	Similar	Different
	1. Tim	We love to travel.	He likes country music.
	2. Benjamin	We like to snuggle with loved ones.	He speaks Spanish.
	3. Maria	We watch *The Simpsons.*	She plays an instrument.
	4. Gail	We love to read.	She doesn't travel much.
	5. Wayne	We lift weights regularly.	He doesn't have any pets.
	6. Heidee	We love to cook.	I don't collect anything.

Ask these questions . . .

➤ How difficult (or easy) was it to share information about yourself with others?

➤ What surprises did you experience finding similarities and differences?

➤ How can we learn more about each other back on the job?

Tips for success . . .

➤ Encourage the participants to not duplicate any answers. If you find a second person with whom you share a love of chocolate, try to find something else you also have in common with that person.

➤ Encourage them to have unrelated Similarities and Differences. For example, if the Similarity is "we both love music," rather than "he likes rap and I don't" as the Difference, try for something unrelated to music altogether.

➤ You may use this activity just to get acquainted or get a meeting started without asking the Debrief questions afterward.

Try these	► Limit similarities and differences to only work-
variations . . .	related items or only personal items.
	► Divide the group into teams of four to six partici-
	pants. Have each team find one thing all members
	have in common and an area in which all mem-
	bers differ. After a few minutes, shuffle the teams,
	and repeat.

For virtual   This activity is not suitable for virtual teams.
teams . . .

SWEET STORIES

This is . . .   An activity in which participants share a story about themselves based on the color of the candy they have in their hands.

The purpose is . . .   Participants learn more about each other and learn to trust each other a little more.

Use this when . . .
- One or more individuals are new to the group.
- Individuals do not know each other very well.
- The group members know each other very well (see variation below).

Materials you'll need . . .
- A large bag of M&Ms®, Skittles®, or other colored candy pieces.

Here's how . . .
1. Have each participant take one candy.
2. Do not let them eat it yet!
3. Let participants take turns sharing with the group a story based on the following code:
   - Blue candy: A time at work when you felt very proud.
   - Green candy: A boss you respected and why.
   - Yellow candy: A reason you are proud to belong to this organization.
   - Brown candy: An embarrassing moment at work.
   - Orange candy: A time at work when you failed (and what you learned).

> ➤ Purple candy: A funny thing that happened to you at work.

> ➤ Red candy: A time at work when you were scared.

4. Now participants can eat the candy.

Ask these questions . . .
➤ Why is it important for us to learn about each other at work?

➤ How difficult (or easy) was it to share information about yourself with others?

➤ How can we learn more about each other back on the job?

Tips for success . . .
➤ Other categories can be used that relate more closely to the workload, organization, or special project.

➤ The stories do not have to be "the most" any-thing—the most embarrassing, the most funny, and so forth. Take that pressure away. Allow participants to relate the kind of story they are comfortable sharing with the group.

➤ If you use a candy other than M&Ms®, be sure to adjust the color coding to match the colors of what you use.

➤ This activity can be repeated. Just ask for different stories! Or start every meeting with one person telling a story. Over time you will hear from everyone.

➤ Limit the length of stories so no one monopolizes the time.

➤ Post the story color code so participants can easily match their candy to the story they need to tell.

Try these variations . . .
➤ Divide larger groups (more than 12 participants) into smaller teams to share their stories with each other.

- ➤ Remove the words "at work" for each color, and get to know each other better personally.
- ➤ Divide the group into small groups of three to five participants. Give them several minutes to share their stories from one color. Select the best story from the team, and share with the larger group.
- ➤ Use only two categories. Toss a coin to determine which story to tell.
- ➤ For the group that knows each other very well, have them tell the stories about each other rather than about themselves.
- ➤ Get to know each other on a personal level along lines such as these: one thing you learned from your parents, why you like your favorite movie, a description of your kitchen at home, a story about pets you have (or have had), and so forth.

For virtual teams . . .

This activity works well for virtual teams.

1. At Step 1, tell participants to have a bag of candies with them. Then select one randomly.
2. Each variation listed can work for a virtual team.

CHAPTER 5

Cooperation: Working Together as a Team

CATCH!

This is . . .   A fast-paced ball-tossing game where participants are encouraged to improve the time it takes to pass the ball around the group.

The purpose is . . .   The group sees that improvements can always be made to a process and that it takes the whole team to make process improvement work.

Use this when . . .

➤ The group needs to be looking to itself (rather than the boss) for ways to improve.

➤ A feeling of arrogance (*"We can't get much better than this!"*) is strong in the group.

➤ Group members are not cooperating with each other as well as they should.

Materials you'll need . . .

➤ A Koosh® ball, beanbag, or similar item that is safe to toss.

➤ A stopwatch, watch, or clock with a second hand.

Here's how . . .

1. Arrange the group in a large circle with everyone standing.
2. Give the ball to anyone.
3. Ask that person to throw the ball to any other person in the circle.
4. The catcher now throws the ball to someone else in the circle.
5. This continues as each participant always throws the ball to someone who has not had it yet.

6. The last one throws the ball back to the participant who had it first. The group has established its Pattern.

7. Have them repeat the same Pattern throwing the ball to the same person, in the same order as they did before. Time them. Their goal is to pass the ball through the Pattern as quickly as possible.

8. If anyone drops the ball, it goes back to the first participant to start again. Time keeps ticking.

9. Announce the time, and ask them how much faster they think they can get.

10. Repeat the Pattern, and time them again.

11. Give them 3 minutes to create a strategy to vastly improve their time again.

12. Repeat the Pattern, and time them again.

For example . . .   There is no appropriate example for this activity.

Ask these questions . . .

> ➤ How did you feel the first time I timed you? On subsequent timings? *(Nervous; energized; competitive; pressured; etc.)*
> ➤ What strategies did you employ to improve your speed? How successful were they?
> ➤ What assumptions or limits did you impose on yourselves? *(We had to stay in the same circle order we were in; We had to catch with our hands [not laps, if sitting]; etc.)*
> ➤ How did you feel when participant X dropped the ball? *(Frustrated; angry; depressed; hopeless; empathetic; etc.)*
> ➤ What was the key to your success?
> ➤ What implication does this have for us back on our jobs?

Tips for **success . . .**	➤ Help them be successful. If they forget who gets the ball next, remind them. Just be careful not to take over leadership for the group.
	➤ Be supportive of whoever drops the ball if the group is not.
	➤ Do not offer suggestions on how to improve; let them struggle with it. An obvious way is for them to rearrange their positions in the circle!
	➤ Watch, and listen to their comments during the activity. Bring up relevant ones during the Debrief.
	➤ Post the rules of the game so participants can refer to them while they play. Be careful not to use words that restrict them from options that do not require actual catching and tossing.
Try these **variations . . .**	➤ Establish two different patterns in the group with two different colored balls. Time them accomplishing both patterns at the same time.
	➤ Form two groups (each with one ball), and time them simultaneously. See if the groups compete more against their own time (which is the stated objective) or against each other's times. Ask how the competitive pressure helps or hinders their efforts on the job.
	➤ Challenge them to reverse their Pattern and still maintain the same or better speed.
	➤ For smaller groups, have them also say their name, a color, a company product, and so forth as they toss the ball.
For virtual **teams . . .**	This activity is not suitable for virtual teams.

1, 2, 3, 4, 5... COUNT OFF

This is . . .   An activity in which participants count off to a number twice the size of the group.

The purpose is . . .   Participants learn to cooperate with each other, have fun, and reinforce camaraderie.

Use this when . . .
- A new group is forming and needs to come together.
- Individuals need to slow down and focus.
- Individuals are not cooperating well as they should.

Materials you'll need . . .
- No materials are necessary for this activity.

Here's how . . .
1. Have the group sit in a large circle.
2. Instruct the group to count to a number that is twice the number of people in the group.
3. Each participant may only say two numbers during the activity.
4. Only one participant may say a number at a time. If two people speak at the same time, the group must start counting again.
5. Each succeeding number must be spoken by a participant who is not sitting next to the one who just spoke.
6. No one may say anything during the activitiy other than one of their two numbers.

Ask these questions . . .	➤ What did you do to be successful?
	➤ How did you feel when the group had to start over? *(frustrated; angry at Joe; relieved it wasn't me who messed up; etc.)*
	➤ How did you feel if you were someone who made the group start over? *(I let the team down; I screwed up; like people were mad at me; etc.)*
	➤ Did you have a leader? How was he or she selected? How did he or she contribute to your success?
	➤ What does this activity tell you about cooperation in our group?
	➤ What implications does this have for us back on the job?
Tips for success . . .	➤ Have them begin immediately after giving instructions; don't give them time to plan anything.
	➤ Don't offer solutions or help—let them figure out what works and what doesn't.
	➤ Watch and listen to comments they make during the activity. Bring up relevant ones during the Debrief.
	➤ If the group struggles, stop the activity and give the members a moment to plan their strategy.
Try these variations . . .	➤ Time the first round. Give them a few minutes to plan; then time a second round.
	➤ Make it more difficult by blindfolding the participants (so they can't give each other visual clues).
	➤ Make it easier by omitting Step 5 and/or Step 6.
For virtual teams . . .	Each variation of this activity works well for virtual teams if audio is available and there are no audio lags between sites.

FLOOR DESIGNS

This is . . . An activity in which participants re-create a hand-drawn picture in a large format on the floor.

The purpose is . . . Participants learn to cooperate with each other, have fun, and reinforce commaradarie.

Use this when . . .
- A new group is forming and needs to come together.
- The group needs to loosen up, have some fun, and laugh.
- Group members are not cooperating with each other as well as they should.

Materials you'll need . . .
- A ream of paper.
- A pen, crayon, or fine-tip marker for each participant.

Here's how . . .
1. Have each participant draw a picture on a blank sheet of paper.
2. Randomly select one drawing.
3. Have the group mimic the drawing on the floor using only the ream of paper (no pens, markers, etc.).

Ask these questions . . .
- What did you do to be successful? (*We let Aisha, the one who drew the picture, tell us how to get it right; We divided the drawing into parts and split the work; etc.*)

> How did you decide how large or small to make the duplication? (*We didn't, it just happened; The size of paper pretty much dictated; We only had this much space; etc.*)

> What got in the way of your success? What might you do differently next time? (*We spent too much time reworking stuff because we didn't plan ahead; We lost a few people as we overengineered the scale; etc.*)

> Did you have a leader? How was he or she selected? How did he or she contribute to your success?

> What does this activity tell you about cooperation in our group?

> What implications does this have for us back on the job?

Tips for success . . .

> The picture they draw at first may be of anything or you may want to specify a theme.

> Conduct this in an area with lots of empty floor space or allow them to use chairs, etc., as part of the drawing.

> Watch and listen to comments they make during the activity. Bring up relevant ones during the Debrief.

> Select a drawing that has some complexity to it or allow the team to do a second or third drawing after successfully completing the first.

> Allow creativity; they may want to fold or rip the paper for a better result.

> For a group larger than eight to ten people, divide the participants into smaller teams of four to eight.

Try these variations . . .

> Blindfold some or all members of the group.

> If more than one team is playing, have them compete to see which team's duplication is more accurate.

- ➤ Set a time limit and have the group compete with the clock to finish before time is up.
- ➤ Rather than duplicate the drawing on the floor, have them turn the drawing into a three-dimensional model by folding, crumpling, and otherwise manipulating the paper into shape.

For virtual teams . . .   This activity is not suitable for virtual teams.

HELIUM STICK

This is . . . A decptively simple activity in which partcipants must lower a pole without losing contact with it.

The purpose is . . . Reinforce the need for commuinication and team-work when addressing group tasks.

Use this when . . .
- ➤ The group needs an energizer before or during a tiring or very long meeting.
- ➤ The group needs to be looking to itself (rather than the boss) for ways to succeed.
- ➤ Group members are not cooperating with each other as well as they should.

Materials you'll need . . .
- ➤ One long, lightweight, and very rigid rod (tent pole, thin wooden dowel, etc.).

Here's how . . .
1. Have the group form two lines facing each other.
2. Participants extend their arms and point their index fingers at about chest height.
3. Place the helium stick (rod) on their extended index fingers, making sure they adjust so the resting helium stick is supported by every index finger at the chest height of the tallest person.
4. Challenge the group to lower the helium stick to the knee height of the shortest person.
5. At no time may any finger lose contact with the helium stick, or the group must start over.

6. The helium stick must rest on the horizontal fingers; none may wrap around or otherwise press down.

Ask these questions . . .

➤ How did you react when the helium stick mysteriously raised while you were trying to lower it?

➤ At what point did you feel frustrated or think that this might be an impossible task? (*When we tried the fifth time and the stick still went up instead of down; When Lee said it was hopeless; etc.*)

➤ How did you finally overcome the tendency for the helium stick to go up? (*Kumar slowed us down and started the lowering cadence; I stopped trying to control everyone by talking louder; etc.*)

➤ What skills did it take to be successful? (*Communication, especially nonverbal; cooperation; listening to each other; slowing down; focusing; etc.*)

➤ What implications does this have for our team back on the job?

Tips for success . . .

➤ The rod works best if it is at least 9″ long for every participant. So a group of 8 would need a rod that is at least 72″ long (8″ × 9″).

➤ This activity works best with 12 or fewer participants. If you have more, get two rods and divide the group.

➤ Use a rod that is as inflexible and lightweight as possible, otherwise it will be too easy to maintain contact.

➤ An odd number of participants will not impact the activity at all. One side will just have an extra participant, but all fingers must still remain on the helium stick.

➤ If the rod is too short, have those on the end only use one finger instead of both.

QUICK TEAM-BUILDING ACTIVITIES FOR BUSY MANAGERS 93

> At first, despite their efforts, the stick will raise. This is because they are so intent on not losing contact that they press upward slightly. Collectively, that raises the stick.

Try these variations . . .
> Make it easier by allowing one (or more) particiant to press down on the stick.
> Make it only slightly easier by having participants only use one finger instead of both.
> Rather than lowering the stick, have them move it across the room or (more difficult) down a flight of stairs while still maintaining the constant contact with every finger involved.

For virtual teams . . .
This activity is not suitable for virtual teams.

PASS THE CARD

This is . . .   A quick moving activity in which participants pass cards from one to another in a relay.

The purpose is . . .   Participants learn that teamwork and the competitive spirit can energize rather than drain them even more than they may feel.

Use this when . . .
- ➤ The group needs an energizer before or during a draining or very long meeting.
- ➤ Individuals would benefit from a shot of competitiveness.
- ➤ Group members are not cooperating with each other as well as they should.

Materials you'll need . . .
- ➤ One deck of playing cards for each team.
- ➤ A prize for the fastest team (optional).

Here's how . . .
1. Divide the group into teams of four to eight participants.
2. Each team sits on chairs in a line side by side.
3. Place a deck of cards on the floor next to the chair at the far right end of each team's line.
4. Give the instructions, and allow teams 5 minutes to plan their strategy.
5. To play, the participant nearest the deck picks up a card with the hand closest to the deck.

6. He then passes the card from one hand to the other, and then to the nearest hand of the participant next to him.
7. The second participant passes that card to her other hand, then on to the nearest hand of the next participant.
8. Play continues like this down the line until the last participant places the card in a pile on the floor next to her with her second hand.
9. No one may hold more than one card at a time.
10. The first team with all cards stacked at the end of their line wins.

For example . . .
As soon as the first participant gets rid of that first card, he can reach down and get the next one to start passing. He does not have to wait for the first card to travel all the way down his line.

Ask these questions . . .
➤ How did you determine your strategy? Did it work?
➤ How did you feel when a participant dropped a card? *(Angry; worried about time; impatient; frustrated; empathetic; etc.)*
➤ Which strategies worked best?
➤ When do we have to be this much in sync at work?
➤ What implications does this have for our team back on the job?

Tips for success . . .
➤ Use this opportunity to mix the group up. Arrange teams so that participants who do not normally work together are on the same team.
➤ As much as possible, have the teams lined up so they can easily see each other. This will increase the competitive nature and also provide distractions!

> Post game rules so participants can refer to them during play.

Try these
variations . . .

> Make this more difficult by blindfolding some (just the first and last?) or all participants.
> Items other than the cards may be used: pennies, paperclips, items unique to your workplace, and so forth.
> Make this more difficult by using pads of sticky notes. Require that the pad be reconstructed at the end of the team line!
> You may also have the cards stacked on chairs or tables at either end of the lines instead of on the floor.

For virtual
teams . . .

This activity is not suitable for virtual teams.

POPCORN

This is . . .   A fun activity in which participants, working in pairs, feed each other pieces of popcorn on a spoon while both are blindfolded.

The purpose is . . .   Participants learn to cooperate with each other, have fun, and reinforce communication skills.

Use this when . . .
> Individuals need to slow down and focus.
> Individuals are not being creative at problem solving.
> The group needs to loosen up, have some fun, and laugh.

Materials you'll need . . .
> A blindfold for each participant.
> A spoon for each participant.
> Popcorn.

Here's how . . .
1. Have the participants pair up.
2. Distribute blindfolds, spoons, and popcorn to everyone.
3. While both are blindfolded, one participant feeds 10 pieces of popcorn to his or her partner on the spoon one at a time.
4. After they are successful, reverse roles and repeat.

For example . . .   There is no appropriate example for this activity.

Ask these questions . . .
> How did you feel when you put on the blindfold? *(Nervous, disoriented, etc.)* Why?

- What happened as you tried to feed each other? *(Popcorn kept blowing off the spoon; She jabbed my nose with the spoon; I had to feel my way; etc.)*
- What ways did you find to communicate, cooperate, and be successful? *(Touch; frequent feedback; overhearing what someone else did that worked; etc.)*
- What implications does this have for us back on the job?

Tips for success . . .

- Prepare by putting small amounts of popcorn in plastic bags for each participant. Some of the popcorn will be dropped, so put more than 10 pieces in each bag!
- Supply something other than popcorn if you know someone is allergic to it.
- Watch to see if anyone cheats with the blindfolds. When is it appropriate to break the rules?

Try these variations . . .

- Easier, and perhaps tastier, would be small candies.
- Have the participants alternate feeding each other one piece of popcorn instead of all 10 in a row.
- Only blindfold one of the pair. Did the sighted person feel pressure to accommodate her partner?
- Divide the group into teams of three or more, and have each team member feed the popcorn to the person on the right simultaneously. This is much more difficult and requires much more cooperation and teamwork. In fact, even without blindfolds this is difficult. Alternatively, have every other person blindfolded.
- Use forks to stab the popcorn, instead of spoons.

For virtual teams . . .

This activity is not suitable for virtual teams.

 PUZZLED

This is . . . An activity in which participants learn, as they assemble a puzzle, that other teams have some pieces they need, and they have pieces others need.

The purpose is . . . Participants see that cooperation across real or perceived team boundaries can be beneficial (sometimes even crucial) for success.

Use this when . . .
- ➤ The members of the group need to cooperate with each other or with the members of other groups to be successful.
- ➤ Competitiveness is hindering team efforts.
- ➤ Individuals are asking the boss to solve their problems for them.

Materials you'll need . . .
- ➤ One children's puzzle for each small group, preferably with 20 to 50 pieces.
- ➤ A puzzle bag (or box or envelope) for each group.
- ➤ Assemble the puzzle bags in advance (without the group knowing you have done this):
  - a. Place all the puzzle pieces for each puzzle in a separate bag.
  - b. Line up the filled bags in front of you.
  - c. Remove two to three pieces from each bag.
  - d. Place each of those pieces in in a different bag.

Here's how . . . 1. Divide the group into teams of three to six participants. There must be the same number of teams as you have bags of puzzles.

2. Give each team a bag of puzzle pieces.
3. Do not disclose that the bags have been tampered with.
4. Tell the participants that their objective is to put the puzzles together in less than 5 minutes.
5. Have them begin.

For example . . .

➤ If they ask for help, decline. Encourage them to use what resources are available to accomplish their objective. Tell them, "All the pieces necessary to accomplish your objective are provided."

➤ If they ask permission to work with other groups, be noncommittal. Say, "You know what your objective is; do what you need to do to achieve it!"

Ask these questions . . .

➤ What assumptions did you make at the beginning of this activity? *(We had all the pieces for our puzzle in this bag; We were in a race; We did not need any outside help; etc.)*

➤ Why did you feel this was a competition? *(Conditioned; my natural style; etc.)*

➤ How did you react when you realized you did not have all the pieces you needed? *(Frustrated; angry; lost; etc.)* How did you deal with it then?

➤ How did you feel when other groups came offering pieces or asking for some of your pieces? *(Imposed upon; go away; rushed; confused; etc.)*

➤ How is this similar to our work? *(We ask you for help when we could solve something ourselves; We see everything as a competition; etc.)*

➤ What implications does this have for you back on your jobs?

Tips for success . . .

➤ Be sure that no two puzzles are exactly the same; otherwise, the value of swapping the pieces may be lost.

- ➤ When the first team discovers they are missing a piece, they may look to you for an explanation. Calmly remind them of their objective (to put the puzzles together), and announce that all the puzzle pieces *are* provided.
- ➤ Do not make the types of encouraging comments that may lead them to believe they are in competition *(Oh, this team is doing well; You guys better hurry up; etc.)*.

Try these variations . . .

- ➤ Replace the puzzles with Lego® building sets (and their instruction sheets) having, preferably, fewer than 50 pieces.
- ➤ Make the puzzles yourself out of thick (or laminated) paper. This is especially good if you want the completed puzzles to say something—quotes or messages that will help you segue into the meeting's main topic or focus.

For virtual teams . . .

This activity is not suitable for virtual teams.

STAR POWER

This is . . .   An activity in which participants form a star shape with a long piece of rope.

The purpose is . . .   Participants learn to cooperate with each other, have fun, and reinforce communication skills.

Use this when . . .
- Individuals are not cooperating well.
- A new group is forming and needs to come together.
- The group needs to loosen up, have some fun, and laugh.

Materials you'll need . . .
- One 40- to 50-foot rope.

Here's how . . .
1. Have all participants pick up the rope.
2. They can move their hands along the rope, but they cannot let go (even briefly) to change places with each other.
3. They must form a balanced five-pointed star with the rope in 10 minutes, with no rope left over at either end.

For example . . .   The star may be just the outline of a star or one in which the lines cross over each other, like a star drawn without a pen ever leaving the paper.

Ask these questions . . .	➤ How does this activity relate to teamwork? *(We had to cooperate; We had to agree on things; We had to support the final outcome; We had to listen to each other; etc.)* ➤ How did you deal with everyone's ideas about the way to proceed? ➤ Did anyone emerge as the leader? How did they function? ➤ How did you handle disagreements? ➤ What implications does this have for us back on the job?
Tips for success . . .	➤ You may want to post a drawing of the star for easy reference. Remember, this will help the team (and you may not want to do that!). ➤ For larger groups (more than 20 participants), form two groups, and have two ropes, or simply use a longer rope. Have at least 2 to 3 feet of length per participant.
Try these variations . . .	➤ Have them try another shape, a letter, a word, or your organization's logo. ➤ Blindfold the participants. If you blindfold them all, make the shape much simpler—a square or triangle will be difficult enough. How did the group learn to "see?" ➤ Require that the activity be accomplished without speaking. How did the group manage to communicate? Or, let some speak and some not. How did the group leverage those who could not speak? ➤ Select a leader, and blindfold only that person. How did the leader and group overcome the restriction?
For virtual teams . . .	This activity is not suitable for virtual teams.

CHAPTER 6

Coping: Dealing with Change

BRIDGES AND TOWERS

This is . . .   An activity in which participants start to build a structure, but are given a different goal or set of resources midway through the activity.

The purpose is . . .   Participants learn how to react to changing goals or resources.

Use this when . . .
- ➤ The group is experiencing lots of change at work.
- ➤ Individuals need to learn to adapt in the moment.
- ➤ The group is resisting change.

Materials you'll need . . .
- ➤ An identical set of building materials for each team.
- ➤ A set of identical items to act as weights.

Here's how . . .
1. Divide the group into teams of three to six, and give each team the same set of materials.
2. Assign each team a different goal, using only the materials supplied. One team must build the tallest free-standing structure. Another must build a bridge with the widest possible span. Another must build a structure that will hold as much weight above the table as possible.
3. Give them 3 minutes to plan (but no construction yet!).
4. Then, let them begin building, announcing that they will have 7 minutes to complete their structures.

5. After a few moments, call time out. Have the teams move away from their places, leave everything behind, and take over another team's project.
6. Tell them to resume building the work in progress before them—aiming to meet that structure's goal.
7. Call time, and measure height, span, and or sturdiness (with weights).

For example . . .
➤ Building material sets may include several straws, a foot of tape, several index cards, a couple of paper clips, children's wooden blocks, plastic interlocking blocks (Lego's®), pipe cleaners, etc.
➤ Weights may be several pads of stickies, golf balls, tennis balls, eggs, identical books, etc.

Ask these questions . . .
➤ How did you react when you switched projects? (*I was frustrated; I was demotivated; I was relieved to have a different and more interesting project; I was confused; etc.*)
➤ What was your reaction to the final result of the project your team had planned but was finished by another team? (*Surprised it turned out better than we thought; disappointed it went differently than we had planned; etc.*)
➤ What strategies did you use to deal with the change in focus? (*We sought help from those who knew—the prior team; We took stock of our resources; We adjusted our definition of success; etc.*)
➤ How could we apply what we used and/or learned back on the job?

Tips for success . . .
➤ Make the initial building assignments random. Write them on a slip of paper and have teams choose a slip.

- If there are more than three teams, duplicate assignments. Just make sure that in Step 5, each team ends up with a different assignment.
- If there are two teams, just omit one of the assignments.
- Take Step 5 after all the teams have a good, solid start on construction, usually 1to 3 minutes after Step 4. Don't wait so long that the structure is almost complete! Better to switch sooner than later.
- Decide beforehand if you will allow them to talk to members of other teams or move resources from team to team and if not, declare it upfront. If either is allowed, perhaps don't mention anything and see if the group attempts either strategy.

Try these variations . . .
- At Step 5, announce that they may not dismantle anything at the new table, and they must still strive to meet their original objective (tallest or widest or strongest structure) with the resources before them.
- At Step 5, have them take their structure with them, and then use the resources left by the prior team to finish their original objective.

For virtual teams . . .

This activity is not suitable for virtual teams.

CHANGE TIME LINE

This is . . .   An activity in which participants learn from major changes they have worked through.

The purpose is . . .   Participants see that, even when changes seem to create problems, they can find ways to overcome and be successful. They will also get to know each other a little better.

Use this when . . .
- The group is experiencing lots of change at work.
- The group lacks confidence to accomplish what is ahead of them.
- You don't have prep time and/or materials for anything more elaborate.

Materials you'll need . . .
- Paper and pens for each participant.

Here's how . . .
1. Give a pen and paper to each participant.
2. Have them each remember five major changes they have experienced in their lifetimes.
3. Participants draw time lines of their lives. Mark when each of the major changes occurred with an "X."
4. Have the participants pair up.
5. Ask them to share with their partner one of the major changes.

6. Post these questions for them to answer as they share:

   a. What made the change difficult?

   b. What was the key to your success in dealing with the change?

   c. How did you feel before, during, and after the change?

   d. How were other changes going on around that time (refer to the time line) affecting your ability to deal with this one?

Ask these questions . . .

➤ How did you feel sharing these experiences with each other? *(I felt a sense of closeness; I realized we have more in common; empathy; etc.)*

➤ What did you learn from how your partner dealt with their major change?

➤ What did you learn about the compounding effect of changes that are close to each other? *(Alone they would be manageable, but together, they seemed overwhelming; The way to deal with one adversely affected the next one; etc.)*

➤ What implications does this have for us back on the job?

Tips for success . . .

➤ Tell the participants that they will be asked to share only one of the major life changes they remember, not all of them. Share only what is comfortable.

Try these variations . . .

➤ After the participants share their experiences, have them pair up with someone else and repeat the activity.

➤ Have the participants share their experiences in teams of three to six. This takes longer, but it will allow them to hear and learn from more experiences than just one or two.

> You may eliminate the time line (and the need for pens and paper). Just have the participants select a major change they have experienced, and then have the dialogue.

For virtual teams . . .

This activity works well for virtual teams.
1. At Steps 1 to 3, have participants work independently in their respective locations.
2. At Step 5, have them discuss with their partners via instant message, phone, etc.
3. Each of the variations listed can work for a virtual team.

INDEX TOWERS

This is . . .	A building activity in which participants use index cards to create a tower.
The purpose is . . .	The group can find creative ways to overcome adversity and be successful, even when changes seem to create problems.
Use this when . . .	➤ The group is experiencing lots of change at work. ➤ Individuals need to be creative about finding efficiencies despite constant change. ➤ Individuals would benefit from a shot of competitiveness.
Materials you'll need . . .	➤ A yardstick or tape measure. ➤ 50 index cards for each team. ➤ A roll (or long piece) of tape for each team. ➤ Small prizes for the winning team (optional).
Here's how . . .	1. Divide the group into teams of three to five participants. 2. Give each team 25 index cards and the tape. 3. Each team has 5 minutes to build the tallest free-standing structure possible using only the materials provided. 4. The structure must stand long enough for you to measure it. 5. After you measure all structures, have the teams destroy them.

6. Announce that you have found that the tape violates health laws and must be forfeited.
7. Now give each team 25 more index cards.
8. Measure the structures and determine the tallest.

Ask these questions . . .

➤ How did you decide on the structure to build each time?

➤ How did you feel when I removed the tape? *(Despair; challenged; frustrated; etc.)*

➤ What ways did you find to be successful in the second round? *(Cooperated more; Found better ways to stack the cards; etc.)*

➤ What implications does this activity have for us back on the job?

Tips for success . . .

➤ Most teams will find a way to build an even taller structure without the tape. If they do not, ask if they think that eventually they could do so (given more time to practice or strategize).

➤ Colored index cards invite the team to aim for aesthetics as well as function.

➤ Be very careful approaching the structures to measure. You don't want to create a slight draft that topples their hard work!

Try these variations . . .

➤ Start with a stapler instead of a roll of tape.

➤ When you take the roll of tape away, replace it with staplers for the second round. Sometimes it is not so obvious whether change is good or bad.

➤ Have a third round in which you increase the number of index cards given to the teams or include some larger index cards. Some change is actually good.

➤ Make the activity go faster by reducing the number of index cards you distribute and then by reducing the time you give them to work.

> ➤ As they are working on their structures, announce that the tape is no longer allowed. After they complete their towers, ask in the Debrief how they adapted to the change in the moment.

For virtual   This activity is not suitable for virtual teams.
teams . . .

MACHINES

This is . . . An activity in which participants create a human machine and then have to change the machine per the customer's request.

The purpose is . . . Participants learn that change can create opportunities for improvement.

Use this when . . .
- ➤ The group is experiencing lots of change at work.
- ➤ Individuals need to be creative about finding solutions during change.
- ➤ You don't have prep time and/or materials for anything more elaborate.

Materials you'll need . . .
- ➤ No materials are necessary for this activity.

Here's how . . .
1. Divide the group into teams of six to ten participants.
2. Give each team 5 minutes to plan a human machine. All participants must be a part of this machine.
3. Watch each team demonstrate its machine
4. Then, select a participant from each machine. Announce that these "machine pieces" are obsolete.
5. The teams now have 3 additional minutes to adjust or reinvent their machines using their selected participant in a new way.

Ask these questions . . .
- ➤ How did you decide on the machine design?
- ➤ How did you handle disagreements in the team?

> How did you feel when I rejected your original design? *(Frustrated and angry with you; Hurt that you singled me out; Anxious to improve the design; etc.)*

> How do we typically react to changes in our own work environment?

> What implications does this have for us back on the job?

Tips for success . . .

> Encourage the teams to be highly creative in their efforts, to use sound effects, and so forth.

> When selecting the participant who will be obsolete, choose the one who has the most pivotal role in the machine. This will force the team to really work on redesigning it.

> Give a 1-minute warning before time is up.

Try these variations . . .

> Impose a purpose or use for the machine, so the teams are then in competition with each other for the best machine for that purpose.

> Require that the planning, assembly, and demonstration be done without speaking.

> After the first machines have been demonstrated, have the teams find a way to incorporate all their machines into one giant machine. This will take the emphasis off of change and place it on creative teamwork and cooperation.

> Have some unusual props available. Assign one or more props to each team. Have them incorporate the prop into their machine design from the beginning or halfway through the activity. Props could include an eggbeater, a broom, a watering can, a silk flower, and so forth.

For virtual teams . . .

This activity is not suitable for virtual teams.

MAKEOVERS

This is . . .	An activity in which participants cut up a picture and then rearrange the pieces into a new image.
The purpose is . . .	Participants see how new and good things can come from changing what was.
Use this when . . .	➤ The group is experiencing lots of change at work. ➤ Individuals need to be creative about finding solutions during change. ➤ Individuals are seeing only the negative aspects of change.
Materials you'll need . . .	➤ At least one picture from a magazine for each participant. ➤ Scissors and glue stick for each participant. ➤ A piece of flipchart paper or other paper for the base of the new picture.
Here's how . . .	1. Allow each participant to select one picture. 2. Have participants cut the picture into small pieces. The pieces should be small enough that the original picture is no longer evident. 3. Each participant uses his or her own pieces to create a new picture. Glue the pieces into a collage on flipchart paper. 4. After 10 minutes, have each participant share his collage and tell what it was before he changed it.
Ask these questions . . .	➤ How did you determine what collage to create? ➤ How did you feel when I gave you the assignment

to create a collage? *(Nervous, because I'm not creative; Anxious to get started; Worried mine might not be good; etc.)*

➤ How do these feeling compare to feelings we have when faced with change at work?

➤ What was the key to your finishing the task successfully?

➤ What implications does this have for us back on the job?

Tips for success . . .

➤ Have an assortment of pictures. The larger the pictures, the better.

➤ Do not give any ideas on what collage to create. They may struggle, but their own ideas will work better for them than any suggestion you may have.

➤ Give a 1-minute warning before the end of time.

Try these variations . . .

➤ Rather than magazine pictures, begin with headlines or other bold words. Have the participants cut the letters up and create a new message with their letters. Or use longer phrases: rather than cutting up letters, cut the words and rearrange them, much like a ransom note might look!

➤ You can assign a specific theme for the collages such as dealing with change, teamwork, listening skills, quality, and so forth.

For virtual teams . . .

Each variation works well for a virtual team if they have video capability at each location.

Z, Y, X, W, V... MY ABC'S

This is . . . An activity in which participants say the alphabet forward and then backward, as quickly as possible.

The purpose is . . . Participants learn how even simple change can affect them.

Use this when . . .
- ➤ The group is experiencing lots of change at work.
- ➤ Individuals need to learn to adapt in the moment.
- ➤ The group is resisting change.

Materials you'll need . . .
- ➤ A stopwatch or other timepiece.

Here's how . . .
1. Have the participants sit in a circle.
2. One participant says A. The person to her right says B. The next one says C, and so on around the circle as many times as necessary until the entire alphabet has been said.
3. Repeat the alphabet while timing how long it takes.
4. Do this again to see if they can improve their time.
5. Challenge the group to be just as fast doing it backward. Start with Z, then Y, then X, etc.
6. Try a few more rounds, timing each one.

Ask these questions . . .
- ➤ What did you think when I asked you to do it backward? (*I didn't think we could be very fast; I was energized by the challenge; I wondered why or what the point was; etc.*)

> How did you feel after the first backward round took as long as it did? (*Surprised it turned out better than we thought; Disappointed it went so slowly; discouraged, etc.*)

> How does this echo the experience we're having back on the job with Change X? (*It's also discouraging; I don't understand why we're doing that either; It's turning out to be more difficult than it seemed at first; etc.*)

Tips for success . . .

> Resist the urge to help them if they get stuck on a letter (otherwise they'll come to rely on you again and again).

> After the first or second round, offer them a moment to strategize before timing them again.

Try these variations . . .

> Instead of the alphabet, use the word order from the Pledge of Allegiance or your organization's mission statement.

> For more competitive groups, have them try to individually recite the alpabet backward.

> Vary the challenge after they get the alphabet backward. Challenge them to only say every other letter, or the last letter then the first letter then the second to the last letter then the second letter (Z, A, Y, B, etc.).

> Have them split into teams. Have the teams compete for the fastest time.

> Have them split into teams. Have them try to individually recite the alphabet backward and time each team member. The team with the fastest average time wins.

For virtual teams . . .

This activity works well for virtual teams if audio is available and there are no audio lags between sites.

1. At Step 1, establish a virtual circle—put the participants in an order they can follow in Steps 2 and beyond.
2. The first three variations listed can work for a virtual team. The fourth variation works well if the teams can be created one at each site.

1,2,3,4... NUMBERS

This is . . .   A fast paced number game in which participants either call numbers out quickly, or they are sent to the end of the line.

The purpose is . . .   Participants learn to cope with rapid-paced changes.

Use this when . . .
- ➤ The group is experiencing lots of change at work.
- ➤ Individuals need to see that minor mistakes are just that: minor!
- ➤ You don't have prep time and/or materials for anything more elaborate.

Materials you'll need . . .
- ➤ No materials are necessary for this activity.

Here's how . . .
1. Arrange the group into a "U" formation.
2. Have them count off down the line so everyone has a number.
3. The first participant begins by calling anyone else's number.
4. Immediately that person must call someone else's number.
5. Play continues like this until someone hesitates or calls an incorrect number (either their own number or a number that is not in the group).

6. That participant goes to the end of the line. She and everyone who was behind her now have a new number.

7. Resume play.

Ask these questions . . .

➤ How did you feel when you made a mistake? *(Like a failure; I let the team down; Disappointed in myself; embarrassed, etc.)*

➤ How did it feel to watch someone else make a mistake? *(Empathy; Glad it wasn't me; angry or frustrated; disappointed; etc.)*

➤ What is our typical reaction when we make minor mistakes at work? (Point out that changes lead to some minor mistakes, and we should not focus on them.)

➤ How did you feel as your number kept changing? How did you feel watching the pressure others were experiencing, but you weren't?

➤ What implications does this have for us on the job?

Tips for success . . .

➤ Have the group set a pace by clapping hands to a beat.

➤ Quicken the pace so everyone "fails" often and the numbers change frequently.

➤ Watch to see if anyone tries deliberately to trip up those at the beginning of the line. Ask why during the Debrief. What causes us to sabotage others?

Try these variations . . .

➤ When a participant makes a mistake, encourage him or her to take a bow, and have the group applaud him or her. Reinforce the concept that learning from minor mistakes is truly a good thing!

➤ Use the alphabet instead of numbers.

For virtual teams . . .

This activity is not suitable for virtual teams.

 # PUZZLED THUMBS

This is . . .   A puzzle activity in which the rules for puzzle assembly change halfway through the exercise.

The purpose is . . .   Participants will experience the value that information has when dealing with change. They will also see that their own reactions to change are normal and manageable.

Use this when . . .
> The group is experiencing lots of change at work.
> Individuals need to be creative about finding efficiencies despite constant change.
> Individuals need to understand that most reactions to change are normal and often take time to work through.
> The group is resisting change.

Materials you'll need . . .
> One children's puzzle for each small group. The best puzzles have a solid frame and border with 15 to 25 pieces.
> A stopwatch, watch, or clock with a second hand.

Here's how . . .
1. Divide the group into smaller teams of two to four participants.
2. Give each team a puzzle. Have them separate all the pieces and place them face up on the table. No puzzle piece may be touching any other puzzle piece to begin.
3. Time the teams assembling their puzzles.
4. Repeat the puzzle assembly two more times; the teams should try to improve their assembly time.

5. Now, inform them that thumbs may no longer be used. Each time a thumb touches a puzzle piece, 1 minute is added to that team's final time.
6. Time the teams assembling their puzzles.
7. Repeat the puzzle assembly two more times; the teams should try to improve their assembly time.
8. After six rounds, compare times and discuss.

Ask these questions . . .

➤ How did you feel about the first three rounds? *(Energized; excited; competitive; foolish making children's puzzles at work; etc.)*

➤ How did you feel about your last three rounds? *(Less excited; Angry with you for prohibiting thumbs; Discouraged; Frustrated with our slower times; etc.)*

➤ How did you react when I told you that you couldn't use your thumbs any more? *(Excited about the challenge; demotivated; discouraged; angry; etc.)*

➤ What if I had explained that you couldn't use your thumbs because we discovered a carcinogen on the puzzle pieces that affected humans ONLY when it touched their thumbs? *(I'd be less angry; Happy you're watching out for us; Angry we had already been exposed; etc.)*

➤ How does having information about changes help you cope at work?

➤ What could have been done to make the last three rounds more productive for you? *(Watch for whether the group focuses on what they could do/control or what you could do/control' pliers or other new tools; etc.)*

➤ What implications does this have back on the job?

Tips for success . . .

➤ As you watch the clock, call out times as the teams finish. They can record their own times. Or, have each team time themselves with their own watches.

> After you announce the thumb rule, listen to their comments. They will often say things such as, "What a stupid rule. This is going to slow us down. . . ." These remarks make for great discussion afterward in the Debrief.

Try these variations . . .

> Tell half the groups the reason for Thumbs Rule and the other half not. Compare the differences in attitudes and times between these groups.
> For competitive groups, keep a running record of best times on a flipchart or board.
> The task can be something other than puzzles—towers of plastic building blocks, houses of cards, lines of dominoes, and so forth.
> Make it more team focused by recording only the time of the slowest team. The teams will learn to share best practices with each other to better everyone's times.
> Switch puzzles after the first three rounds.
> After six rounds, remove the puzzle frame for another three rounds (still not allowing thumbs), or blindfold the participants. These more difficult changes will simulate the feeling of constant change that many feel at work. Afterward, discuss how the changes compounded reactions. What can be done to minimize the negative impact of that phenomenon?
> Blindfold only one person on each team, but allow only that person to still use his or her thumbs. How did the teams work around the blindness and leverage the available thumbs?

For virtual teams . . .

This activity is not suitable for virtual teams.

SQUARES

This is . . .	An activity in which participants must switch standing on an ever-decreasing number of squares.
The purpose is . . .	Participants learn to think outside the box when change happens.
Use this when . . .	➤ The group is experiencing lots of change at work. ➤ Individuals are holding on to the old way of doing things. ➤ Individuals need to be more creative in their responses to change.
Materials you'll need . . .	Large (12″ × 12″ or so) squares.
Here's how . . .	1. Place all the squares on the floor, randomly spaced. 2. Ask all participants to stand on "a square" with both feet in the square. 3. Review the rules: Everytime you say SWITCH, they must immediately move to a new square. And, they cannot continue unless everyone has both feet on a square. 4. Call out SWITCH. Everyone will move to a new square. 5. Repeat Step 4 one or two more times. 6. Continue repeating Step 4, but now start pulling up a square after each round. Eventually, there

will be fewer squares than there are partcipants. When this happens, one person will not be standing on a square.

7. Remind the group of the rule "we cannot continue unless everyone has both feet on a square" and wait for them to address the situation. (Likely, someone will allow a participant to share their square.)

8. Continue repeating Step 6. Eventually, they will run out of space to share on the remaining squares. Again, remind them of the rules and then wait for them to address the situation.

9. If they get stuck, point out that you will continue to remove paper squares, and ask how they think the activity will end if they keep acting on the same assumptions. The first assumption they abandoned was that only one person could stand on a square. Ask them what other assumptions can they alter and still be successful following the rules of the game.

10. Eventually, one participant will realize that "square" doesn't have to be one of the paper squares on the floor. When they stand elsewhere, merely ask, "Are you standing with both feet on a square?" When they answer yes, continue calling SWITCH and removing more paper squares until none are left.

For example . . . The materials can be newspaper, flipchart paper, fabric, cardboard, etc., but they must be square.

Ask these questions . . . ➤ How did you feel when there was one less paper square on the floor than number of participants? (*I didn't want to be the odd one out; I felt pressure to get one of the remainging squares; etc.*)

➤ How did you react when I reminded you that the game couldn't continue without eveyone on a square? (*there must be some trick to this; we'll have to share; I'm glad I'm not the odd one out; etc.*)

➤ How did you feel when I challenged your assumptions a second time? (*less confident because the answer wasn't as obvious that time; baffled; angry you didn't give us any hints; etc.*)

➤ How were you reacting to the changes I kept introducting? (*with fear; felt challenged; anxious; etc.*)

➤ What did you learn about how you react to change? And, about how the group reacts?

➤ What assumptions are we holding on to that may be getting in the way of change we're experiencing on the job?

Tips for success . . .

➤ Post the rules for this activity for easier reference. Always say "a square" and never "the square" or "a newspaper square" so participants are not locked into old-school thinking because of your words

1. Everyone must have both feet on a square.
2. When I say SWITCH, everyone must move to a new square immediately.
3. We cannot continue the game unless everyone has both feet on a square.

➤ Be prepared to see some real creativity, and don't be too obsessed with a perfect square. For example, the seat of some chairs are close to being square and someone may stand on one. Also, there is no rule that prevents them from taking some pencils and outlining a square on the floor or considering a square of tile or carpet as valid (so long as both feet fit in that square).

➤ Be careful not to lead them too much at Step 7 (just remind them of the rules, nothing more!)

and Step 9. Resist that urge, and let them struggle for a bit. The learning is much greater if they find it than if you give it.

Try these variations . . .

➤ Make it more difficult by skipping Step 9 and just let them come to their own conclusions without any help. This may take a few extra minutes. In the Debrief ask how assumptions got in the way.

➤ Add some fun to the activity by playing music while they are switching. Like the children's game Musical Chairs, when you stop the music they must find themselves on a square.

For virtual teams . . .

This activity is not suitable for virtual teams.

CHAPTER 7

Creativity: Solving Problems Together

 **BALLOON SCULPTURES**

This is . . .	A fun activity in which participants create a balloon sculpture that reflects the team.
The purpose is . . .	The group members openly express their commitment to the team.
Use this when . . .	➤ A new team is forming and needs to come together. ➤ Creative thinking is not happening very much. ➤ Individuals are not cooperating well. ➤ The group needs a shot in the arm of team spirit.
Materials you'll need . . .	➤ One long balloon (the kind circus clowns use) for each participant and some extras. ➤ A balloon pump (optional but highly recommended; these are often included with the purchase of the balloons).
Here's how . . .	1. Give each participant one balloon. 2. Have the entire team create a balloon structure that reflects their commitment to the team.
For example . . .	Balloons linked together may suggest interdependence, balloons touching may represent connectivity, balloons on the bottom may suggest supporting others, and so forth.
Ask these questions . . .	➤ How does this activity relate to teamwork? *(We had to work together; We had to agree on things;*

We had to support the final outcome; Each balloon reflected our individual input; etc.)

➤ How did you deal with everyone's ideas about the sculpture?

➤ How did you handle disagreements?

➤ What implication does this have for us back on the job?

Tips for success . . .

➤ Have the balloons blown up before the activity if possible.

➤ Have extra balloons ready for the few that will break.

➤ Do not blow the balloons up completely. Leave an inch or more to allow for bending and stretching.

➤ Watch for team behaviors during the activity that you can bring up during the Debrief.

Try these variations . . .

➤ If the group consists of intact work teams, divide the group into those teams. Have them each create a sculpture. Then have them share their creation with the others. If there are fewer than five participants in a team, you may need to make more balloons available for them.

➤ Have the team think of a team name that complements their sculpture and reinforces their commitment to the team.

➤ Use building blocks instead of balloons. Give each participant five or more blocks.

➤ Instead of balloons, use your organization's own products or items to which your group can particularly relate.

For virtual teams . . .

This activity is not suitable for virtual teams.

CARD STACK

This is . . . An activity in which participants organize a random stack of cards into the best arrangement possible.

The purpose is . . . Participants learn to cooperate with each other, have fun, and reinforce communication skills.

Use this when . . .
- ➤ Individuals need to understand the value of being flexible with plans and strategies.
- ➤ Creative problem solving is not happening very much.
- ➤ Individuals are not cooperating well.

Materials you'll need . . .
- ➤ A set of 16 random playing cards for each team.

Here's how . . .
1. Divide the group into teams of three to five participants.
2. Give each team a set of 16 playing cards.
3. Have the teams lay out all their cards in a grid (four rows and four columns).
4. The object is for them to reduce the 16 cards down to one stack, or the smallest number of stacks possible.
5. Explain these rules:
   a. A card (or stack) may be moved any distance horizontally or vertically, but never diagonally.
   b. It must always end its move on top of another card (or stack) that is the same rank or suit. It can never take an empty space.

c. Once a card is placed on top of another card, the resulting stack is moved as one unit driven by its top card (all cards below become irrelevant for the remainder of the game).

6. Allow the teams 10 minutes to play.

For example . . . A 2 of diamonds may move horizontally 1 space to cover a stack topped by a 4 of diamonds (matching suit) or vertically 3 spaces to cover a 2 of clubs (matching rank). It cannot be moved diagonally for any reason. Once the 2 is moved to cover the 4, that 4 becomes irrelevant. The new stack, consisting of the 2, the 4, and cards below the 4, is now moved as one unit based on the top card, the 2 of diamonds. Or, the reverse move could have been made. The stack topped with a 4 of diamonds could have been moved horizontally to cover the 2 of diamonds. The resulting stack, with the 2 of diamonds on the bottom, is now moved according to its top card, the 4 of diamonds.

Ask these questions . . .
- ➤ How close were you to the goal of one final stack?
- ➤ What affected your final result? Since each set of cards was different, how did available resources affect the outcome? Does this happen at work?
- ➤ How did you deal with everyone's ideas about the way to proceed? (*We all had to agree before a move was made; Tim knew what he was doing, so we just let him drive it; etc.*)
- ➤ How does this activity relate to teamwork? (*We had to cooperate; We had to agree on a process; We had to listen to each other; etc.*)
- ➤ Did anyone emerge as the leader? How did he or she function?
- ➤ How did you handle disagreements?
- ➤ What implications does this have for us back on the job?

Tips for success . . .	➤ Post the rules so participants can refer to them during play.
	➤ Help the teams remember that once a card is on top of one or more other cards, that card stack moves as one unit. Only the top card remains relevant to play.
	➤ Stacks can move on top of other stacks to create a new stack. Again, only the top card remains relevant to play.
	➤ Play with a set of cards beforehand so you get a sense of the card movements.
Try these variations . . .	➤ Give the teams exactly the same set of 16 cards. Increase the competition by announcing the exact configuration of cards from which all teams begin play.
	➤ Use more cards for greater difficulty, fewer cards to finish in less time (but using fewer than 12 cards does not allow the team to grasp the learning points).
	➤ Allow one diagonal move per game. How does the added "flexibility" impact the final outcome? Not all change is bad!
	➤ Have the teams remember how they configured their cards the first time (take a picture with a smart phone). Play another round, and see if they can improve their results. Add a level of change by having one participant from each team move to a different team for the second round. How did this new pair of eyes affect the results?
For virtual teams . . .	This activity is not suitable for virtual teams.

CONSULTANTS

This is . . . An activity that allows participants to give each other advice on how to handle work problems.

The purpose is . . . Participants get help solving problems or get creative ideas for dealing with work issues.

Use this when . . .
- ➤ Individuals are not helping or supporting each other very well.
- ➤ Individuals need to see the value of others' input and help.
- ➤ You don't have prep time and/or materials for anything more elaborate.

Materials you'll need . . .
- ➤ Paper and pens for each participant.

Here's how . . .
1. Each participant writes one problem or concern he or she currently faces at the top of a piece of paper. Give the group 2 minutes to do this.
2. Have everyone pass their papers to the participant on their left.
3. Each participant has 1 minute to read the problem in front of him or her and write some advice.
4. Pass the papers again, and repeat as often as time allows.
5. Return the papers to the original owners.

For example . . .	Problem:
	➤ I have trouble making eye contact when giving negative feedback.
	Solutions:
	➤ Try practicing in a mirror.
	➤ Make sure your feedback is not attacking or otherwise making the person feel defensive; then maybe it won't be so hard.
	➤ Role-play with a friend.
	➤ Remember, it may not be as negative as you fear it is!
	➤ Watch how easily Patti does it, she's a pro!
Ask these questions . . .	➤ How many got one or more ideas that will truly help them resolve their issue?
	➤ How did you feel having to give advice? *(On the spot, at a loss, honored and respected, pressured to come up with something fantastic, etc.)*
	➤ Why do we not ask each other for help more often? *(Do not want to impose, think we have to have the answer ourselves, do not trust others will have any good ideas, etc.)*
	➤ What implications does this have for us back on the job?
Tips for success . . .	➤ Encourage partial advice. If a participant cannot think of advice, he or she can write a few words of encouragement and support or suggest another resource to go to for advice.
	➤ The advice does not have to be revolutionary or complete. Usually the first thought that comes up is a good one. Even if it is not a very good one, it may prompt someone else to come up with a better one!

Try these
variations . . .

➤ Sit in a circle. The first participant explains briefly his or her problem or concern. All other participants take turns offering advice out loud. The first participant cannot say a word (to explain why something will not work, for example)—just listen and thank the others for their help.

➤ This activity can work for creative idea generation rather than problem solving. For example, where should we go for our holiday dinner, how can we increase community service participation, and so forth.

For virtual
teams . . .

This activity works well for virtual teams.

1. Rather than writing on paper, have participants write their problem or concern in an email at Step 1.
2. Publish a list of participants.
3. At Step 2, each participant sends their email to the person whose name follows their own on the list.
4. At Step 4, again send the email to the person whose name follows your own on the list.
5. A variation: Participants put their advice at Step 3 in an attachment to the email so others don't see what was written before them. Each round another attachment is added until the email returns to its original owner.
6. Each variation listed can work for a virtual team.

IMPROVE THIS

This is . . .	A very quick activity in which participants try to improve their seating arrangement with no specific goal in mind.
The purpose is . . .	Participants learn that objectives or goals must be specific; that assumptions left unchecked can sabotage an effort.
Use this when . . .	➤ Individuals need to see the value of setting clear and specific goals.
	➤ Individuals are making assumptions or not asking questions for clarification.
	➤ You don't have prep time and/or materials for anything more elaborate.
Materials you'll need . . .	➤ No materials are necessary for this activity.
Here's how . . .	1. Announce to the group that they have exactly 60 seconds to improve their seating arrangement.
	2. Do not give any further instruction. Look at a clock and tell them to begin . . . now!
	3. If they ask for clarification, simply repeat the original instructions.
	4. Stop the activity after 60 seconds and discuss.
Ask these questions . . .	➤ Did you meet your objective? How do you know? *(Yes, because I am closer to the window; No, because I'm not sure what the objective was; I'm not sure; etc.)*

> What was your objective? Was it clear? *(If they think it was clear, ask them to define "improve," and then show how it could have meant to get more people up front, or to get in a better circle, or to sit boy–girl–boy–girl, etc.; to show there were assumptions made; etc.)*

> Did you seek clarification? Why not? Or what happened when you tried?

> How does this situation relate to the workplace? *(We often try to accomplish things when we are not clear on the real goal or the specific criteria for success; We often don't ask for clarification, and if we do, we don't press until we get what we truly need to succeed; etc.)*

> What can we do to prevent this kind of thing happening back on the job?

Tips for success . . .

> After giving the instructions, do not ask if there are any questions. Look at the clock to discourage their questions. It is amazing how quickly anyone wanting clarification will back off if the source appears elusive. Usually, the pressure of the group will discourage anyone from not moving quickly.

> If they directly ask for clarification, say, "You determine for yourselves what "improve" means. You are all adults. It seems pretty obvious." During the Debrief, point out how similar this is to responses back on the job. ("You figure out what better customer service is; that's what you're paid for!")

> Do not be surprised (and do not stop them!) if they start moving tables and chairs to "improve" their seating arrangement.

> During the Debrief, do not beat them up for their behavior. Remember, you set them up. The purpose is to show them how often their work environment sets them up like this, and how they typically respond.

> As they rearrange themselves, listen to their comments. They will say things such as, *"I don't know what she wants, but let's try this. . ."* Bring these up (without pointing at who said what) during the Debrief.

**Try these
variations . . .**

> This does not have to be done at the beginning of a meeting. Done at any other time, it can also energize the group that is lagging a bit.
> For more focused and in-depth learning, you can give them a specific work goal and have them improve it. For example, Improve order processing is vague, as stated; improving it will be difficult without getting clarity about what, specifically, needs to be improved, and whether that's part of the process itself, or the result of the process.
> After doing this activity as outlined, try variations wherein you are explicit about what you want them to accomplish, and see how closely the group meets your expectations. Let others take a turn being specific with the goal.

**For virtual
teams . . .**

This activity is not suitable for virtual teams.

MAGIC CARPET RIDE

This is . . .	An activity in which participants flip a sheet over while all standing on it.
The purpose is . . .	Participants learn to cooperate with each other, have fun, and reinforce communication skills.
Use this when . . .	➤ The group has difficulty dealing with conflict over processes or methods. ➤ Creative problem solving is not happening very much. ➤ Individuals are not cooperating well.
Materials you'll need . . .	➤ One large flat sheet or table cloth or simliar (80″ × 90″ or larger).
Here's how . . .	1. Spread out the sheet on the floor. 2. Have everyone stand on the sheet (where they stand doesn't matter, as long as both feet are on the sheet). 3. Challenge the team to flip over the sheet without anyone touching the floor and without anyone being lifted off the sheet.
Ask these questions . . .	➤ What strategy did you use to be successful? ➤ What other strategies may have worked? How did you select the one you used?

> How were differences of opinion about how to proceed handled in your team?
> Did you have a leader? How was he or she selected?
> When someone on your team thought he or she knew how to proceed, how did he or she behave? How did you respond to that?
> What implications does this have for us back on the job?

Tips for success . . .

> This activity works best with 12-18 participants for a sheet approximately 80″ × 90″. For smaller teams, use a smaller sheet. For large groups, use a larger sheet, or divide the group into teams of 12 to 18, with separate sheets.
> Have participants take their shoes off (especially high heels) for safety.
> Watch and listen to comments they make during the activity. Bring up relevant ones during the Debrief.
> You can do this activity outdoors on pavement or on grass (perferable).
> Refrain from rushing the group (do not time this activity), as the added pressure may result in injuries.

Try these variations . . .

> Use more than one size sheet. Start with the largest. After the team has successfully managed that one, use a smaller one. In the Debrief, ask them to compare strategies.
> Tape flip chart pages together to make one large sheet of paper approximately 80″ × 90″. Then conduct the same activity. It becomes much more difficult with the prospect of paper tearing. You may allow accidental rips as long as the other rules hold (no stepping on the floor and no lifting any-one) and eventually the paper is turned over and

lays flat and in its original shape beneath the team. Or, make it even more difficult by not allowing any rips or tears.

➤ Rather than have them turn the sheet over, have them fold it in half (thus cutting their standing area by 50 percent). Then fold it in half again. This is particularly good for smaller groups as the first round will be easy, but it will get more challenging thereafter.

➤ Give them a time limit to add pressure to the challenge. Perhaps give them an opportunity to improve their time with a second round.

For virtual teams . . . This activity is not suitable for virtual teams.

ONE-WORDED STORIES

This is . . .   A story telling activity in which participants construct a story together by contributing one word at a time.

The purpose is . . .   Participants practice cooperating and making each other look good.

Use this when . . .
- Individuals are not cooperating well.
- Individuals are focusing too much on themselves.
- You don't have prep time and/or materials for anything more elaborate.

Materials you'll need . . .
- No materials are necessary for this activity.

Here's how . . .
1. Explain that the group will create a story together, one word at a time.
2. Have the group sit in a circle or a formation in which each person will take a turn.
3. The word used must be as interesting as possible, and it must make the word of the preceding participant work as well as possible.
4. Select one participant to demonstrate how "Once upon a time. . ." might come out with each of you alternating saying those words.

5. After the story is over, try another one or two (the group will get better at this).

For example . . .

Participant 1: "Once"
Participant 2: "upon"
Participant 3: "a"
Participant 4: "time"
Participant 5: "my"
Participant 6: "uncle"
Participant 7: "and"
Participant 8: "his"
Participant 9: "ugly. . ."

Ask these questions . . .

➤ How many felt the person after you said the "wrong" word, because that was not what you meant to have come out? How did that make you feel? *(Angry; frustrated; critical; etc.)*
➤ How would you compare the collective story of the group with what you may have come up with on your own? *(It was more creative and original; It made less sense; It was more fun; etc.)*
➤ Who did not like where the story went? Why not? What could you have done had this been a work situation?
➤ Which story was the best? Why?
➤ What implications does this have for us back on the job, especially when someone does not understand what you intended?

Tips for success . . .

➤ Keep the pace moving along quickly, or the flow of story will be lost repeatedly.
➤ End the story when it feels like it has run its course, or the energy and enthusiasm for that one has waned.
➤ Encourage participants to speak loudly and very clearly.

Try these	➤ To keep the story moving, allow participants the

Try these variations . . .
➤ To keep the story moving, allow participants the option of pointing to the next person when they want to pass. Afterward, ask how the group felt about those who passed. Did anyone pass more than others? How does the group interpret that behavior? Are there some who "pass" at work more often than others?

➤ To encourage teamwork, allow other participants to offer to take someone's turn if they hesitate. Afterward, ask the how the group felt about those who offered help. Did anyone hesitate more than others? Did anyone jump to the rescue more than others?

➤ Use paper. Have each participant start a poem with one line. Pass to the left. Add a line that rhymes. Pass to the left four more times. Read the poems out loud.

➤ Don't take turns at all. Let whoever wants to add a word do so. Did someone dominate? Did anyone not participate?

➤ Use flipchart paper. Each participant adds their word to the page. This makes it easier for them to remember the context as the story develops.

For virtual teams . . .
This activity works well for virtual teams.

1. Establish an order for participants to follow as they build the story together. This will avoid people talking over each other.

2. A variation: Don't take turns telling the story. Let whoever wants to add a word do so. Did someone dominate? Did anyone not participate?

3. A variation: Using email, have each participant start a poem with one line. Pass to the next person on the list and add a line that rhymes. Pass two more times. Read the poems aloud.

PAPER SHUFFLE

This is . . .   An activity in which participants put a newspaper in numerical or page order after it has been shuffled.

The purpose is . . .   Participants learn to cooperate with each other, have fun, and reinforce communication skills.

Use this when . . .
- ➤ Individuals are not cooperating well.
- ➤ A new group is forming and needs to come together.
- ➤ The group needs to loosen up, have some fun, and laugh.

Materials you'll need . . .
- ➤ One newspaper with all pages completely shuffled and out of order for each team.
- ➤ Small prizes for the winning team (optional).

Here's how . . .
1. Divide the group into teams of four to six participants.
2. Give each team one newspaper, completely shuffled.
3. Have the team sort and reorganize the newspaper back into its original order.

Ask these questions . . .
- ➤ How does this activity relate to teamwork? *(We had to cooperate; We had to agree on a process; We had to listen to each other; etc.)*
- ➤ How did you deal with everyone's ideas about the way to proceed?
- ➤ Did anyone emerge as the leader? How did he or she function?
- ➤ How did you handle disagreements?

> What implications does this have for us back on the job?

Tips for success . . .

> Use an identical newspaper for each team. If you use other materials, make sure the number of pages given to each team is equal.
> Do not give any suggestions or advice before or during the task. Let the team members figure things out for themselves.

Try these variations . . .

> Use pages ripped from an old book, but cut off the page numbers first!
> Use a deck of cards instead of newspapers. Indicate what order the suits must be in.
> Use a long document from your organization, such as a procedures manual.
> Do not allow the participants to speak during this activity.
> If the group is too small to form teams, time the group performing the task. Then reshuffle the paper and see if they can improve their time.
> A follow-up activity for fun and to build camaraderie is to have each team use their newspaper and some tape to create a costume for one of their teammates. The teams can compete for most original, most funny, most beautiful, and so forth.

For virtual teams . . .

This activity is not suitable for virtual teams.

CHAPTER 8

Z, Y, X, W, V... Teamwork: Appreciating and Supporting Each Other

BLAME GAME

This is . . .	A quick standstill activity in which participants try to determine who moved first and then assign blame.
The purpose is . . .	Participants see that everyone is responsible for group behavior.
Use this when . . .	➤ Individuals blame others for group problems that they also influence. ➤ Energy is being wasted finding culprits and scapegoats. ➤ You don't have prep time and/or materials for anything more elaborate.
Materials you'll need . . .	➤ No materials are necessary for this activity.

Here's how . . .	1. Arrange the group in a large circle, with everyone standing.
	2. Find your Idol:
	   a. You begin by pointing to someone in the circle. Keep pointing.
	   b. That participant now points to someone else and keeps pointing.
	   c. Continue until everyone is pointing at someone else, and the last participant then points at you.

        d. Stop pointing (drop your hands) and fix your
           eyes on the participant you were pointing at.
           That participant becomes your Idol.
     3. Explain that the objective is to watch your Idol
        closely and copy his or her every action.
     4. Now ask the group to stand perfectly still. No one
        may move *unless* his or her Idol does. And if his or
        her Idol moves (twitches, coughs, blinks, etc.), he
        or she is to mimic that movement exactly and
        then be still again.
     5. Begin the game and play for several minutes.

Ask these   ➤ We were supposed to stand still—what happened?
questions . . .   (Expect some participants immediately to start
                      blaming their Idol for moving.)

                    ➤ Who knows who started the movement? (Allow
                      for some accusations; inevitably it will be difficult
                      or impossible to pinpoint who really started each
                      movement.)

                    ➤ How much does it matter who started it, once it
                      got started?

                    ➤ How much energy do we spend looking for
                      scapegoats?

                    ➤ How are we to blame for perpetuating certain
                      behaviors that eventually become team norms?
                      What examples of this do we have here at work?

                    ➤ What implications does this have for us back on
                      the job?

Tips for   ➤ Small movements are bound to happen. When
success . . .   they do, the movement will be duplicated
                      around the group endlessly. Usually it will
                      be exaggerated.

                    ➤ If the movement gets out of hand, just stop the
                      game, refocus everyone, and start again.

Try these	➤ Designate one participant as "where the buck
variations . . .	stops." When movement starts and moves around
	the group, that participant will NOT repeat it.
	This variation is effective after a few rounds of
	the regular activity. Ask how much influence one
	person can have in affecting team behavior.

For virtual   This activity is not suitable for virtual teams.
teams . . .

BUT NOTHING (FEEDBACK)

This is . . .   A quick verbal activity in which participants give each other personal feedback using "but. . ."

The purpose is . . .   Participants learn how easily "but. . ." can interfere with constructive feedback by creating defensiveness, even when they mean well. They will also learn to replace "but. . ." with "and. . ."

Use this when . . .
- ➤ Feedback is not being received very well.
- ➤ Individuals feel like others are not listening with open minds.
- ➤ You don't have prep time and/or materials for anything more elaborate.

Materials you'll need . . .
- ➤ No materials are necessary for this activity.

Here's how . . .
1. Have the participants pair up.
2. Each participant has 30 seconds to think of something she likes about the other's outfit and one way the outfit could be improved.
3. The first participant tells the other what she likes first, then says, "but. . ." and finishes the sentence with how it could be even better.
4. The other participant then does the same to the first participant.

5. Now have each participant repeat what she just said, replacing "but" with "and."

For example . . .
"I like that tie, but it would bring out your blue eyes better if it was red."
"I like that tie, and it would bring out your blue eyes better if it was red."
"That is a nice dress, but you would look even more professional if you had earrings, too."
"That is a nice dress, and you would look even more professional if you had earrings, too."

Ask these questions . . .
➤ How did it feel to hear "but?" *(Annoying; defensive; insincere; etc.)* How did it feel to hear "and?" *(Helped; respected; supported; etc.)*
➤ What does "but" usually mean? *(Disregard what you just heard, because here is the real truth.)*
➤ Why do we say "but" so often when giving suggestions or feedback?
➤ What implications does this have for us back on the job?

Tips for success . . .
➤ Share an example to give participants a sense of how the statements should sound.
➤ Make sure all pairs have finished their "but" statements before giving the cue to make the "and" statements.
➤ Point out that the word "but" usually negates everything that precedes it.

Try these variations . . .
➤ The more personal the feedback, the better. If the group is uncomfortable giving feedback on each other's outfits, though, select something else, such as the coffee in the lunchroom, a movie they have both seen, and so forth.

- After the meeting, ask for feedback on the meeting without the "but." *(I liked that we had an agenda,* and *next time I hope we can stick to it better.)*
- If the group is comfortable giving feedback to each other already, have them do it on their recent job performance rather than their outfit.
- Add an element of fun to this activity by starting with participants making something creatively (with clay, markers, balloons, building blocks, etc.), and then give the feedback to each other about the creation rather then their outfits.

For virtual teams . . . This activity works for virtual teams. At Step 2, if video is not available, have participants send a selfie to each other or comment on something they both know about (e.g., your organization's IT help desk, the company newsletter, etc.). Each variation listed can work for a virtual team using one of the alternatives above.

BUT NOTHING (IDEAS)

This is . . .   A quick, verbal activity in which participants give each other feedback on their ideas using "yes, but. . ."

The purpose is . . .   Participants learn how easily "yes, but. . ." can shut down communication and creativity, even if well intentioned. They will also learn to replace "yes, but. . ." with "yes, and. . ."

Use this when . . .

➤ Ideas are being shot down frequently; creativity is being stifled.

➤ Individuals feel like others are not listening with open minds.

➤ You don't have prep time and/or materials for anything more elaborate.

Materials you'll need . . .

➤ No materials are necessary for this activity.

Here's how . . .

1. Have the participants pair up.
2. Each pair is to plan a vacation together (money is no object).
3. One partner starts by suggesting something to the other.
4. The other responds by saying, "Yes, but. . ." and finishes her sentence.

5. The first partner then responds by saying, "Yes, but. . ." and finishes his sentence.
6. The conversations continue back and forth this way for 2 minutes.
7. Then, have the same pairs do the same thing with only one change—each sentence must begin with "Yes, and. . ."
8. The conversations continue this way for 2 minutes.

For example . . .

"I want to go someplace warm."
"Yes, but let's make sure it's not Florida."
"Yes, but Puerto Rico could be nice."
"Yes, but I hope one of us speaks Spanish."
"Yes, but we could bring a dictionary, if necessary."
"I want to go someplace warm."
"Yes, and let's make sure it's not Florida."
"Yes, and St. Martin could be nice."
"Yes, and I hope one of us speaks French."
"Yes, and we could bring a dictionary, if necessary."

Ask these questions . . .

➤ How did it feel to hear "but?" *(Annoying; defensive; competitive; etc.)* And how did it feel to hear "and?" *(Accepted; listened to; respected; etc.)*
➤ Did you get along further with your plans during the first or second round? Why?
➤ Why do we say "yes, but. . ." so often? *(It is ingrained in us; The "but" allows us to disagree without being disagreeable; etc.)*
➤ When is "yes, but. . ." useful or appropriate?
➤ What implication does this have for us back on the job?

Tips for success . . .

➤ Read the examples above to give participants a feel for how the conversation might go.
➤ Encourage them to keep the conversation moving. They are not planning a real vacation, so they do not have to be accurate, precise, or realistic.

> The second dialogue does not have to duplicate word for word the first dialogue.

Try these variations . . .

> Ask the Debrief questions after the first round of "buts" while the team's thoughts and feelings are still fresh.
> Plan a party, family reunion, or any other elaborate event that might be fun.
> Start to plan an actual work related function (picnic, fund raising drive, etc.)
> Divide the participants into small groups instead of pairs. The "Yes, but. . ." conversation goes around the circle.

For virtual teams . . .

This activity works for virtual teams. At Step 2, participants can discuss their vacation on private phone lines or via instant messaging. Each variation listed can work for a virtual team using one of the alternatives above.

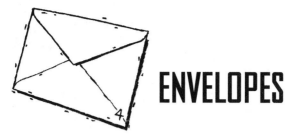

ENVELOPES

This is . . .
An activity in which team members appreciate each other's contributions by offering intangible thank yous.

The purpose is . . .
Participants give and receive appreciation for individual and group efforts.

Use this when . . .
- ➤ A significant project or work effort has been completed, and you want to celebrate the success.
- ➤ Individuals need to recognize and appreciate what's going well among themselves.
- ➤ Periodically, to have the team continually reinforce their collective and individual contributions.

Materials you'll need . . .
- ➤ One envelope for each participant.
- ➤ One slip of paper for each participant.
- ➤ Pens.

Here's how . . .
1. Have each participant write their name on a slip of paper, fold it, and seal it in a blank envelope.
2. Have them write the last digit of their social security number in a corner of the envelope.
3. Shuffle the envelopes and pass out one to each participant. Have them check the digit to ensure they did not get their own envelope. Do not open envelopes yet!
4. Have them think of some intangible way that they would like to thank the coworker named in the

envelope (without knowing who it is yet), and write that on the front of the envelope.

5. Invite them to open the envelope they have and announce to the group what they offered, and then to whom.

For example . . .
Intangible thank yous may be: I'll pick up (not pay for!) your lunch any day of your choosing this month; you may use my parking space for one week; use of my umbrella next time it rains and you don't have one; I'll save a seat for you at the next all-associates meeting so you don't have to get their more than a few minutes early; etc.

Ask these questions . . .
➤ How difficult (or easy) was it to offer thanks to an anonymous coworker?
➤ Why is important for us to do things to say thank you rather than just buy things?
➤ How would your offer have been different if you knew whom you were going to give it to?

Tips for success . . .
➤ Don't offer too many ideas as examples or they may have trouble thinking of their own.
➤ If someone gets their own envelope, gather, re-shuffle, and redistribute them all.
➤ Don't rush them. Bettter to be patient and have them write something truly meaningful, then to just slap something down.

Try these variations . . .
➤ Stop the activity at Step 4. Proceed through the rest of the meeting and end the meeting with Step 5. This will give them time to really ponder their offer.
➤ Do Step 1 yourself, skip Step 2. At Step 5, if some-one has their own envelope, they are then expected to do what they wrote for someone outside of the team whom the team agrees should be recognized.

> ➤ Stop after Step 3. Have participants take their envelopes, open them later and then do something nice for the person who's envelope they got. At the next meeting, report back to the group what happened.

For virtual teams . . .   This activity works well for virtual teams.

1. Skip Steps 1-3. Start by having each participant do Step 4, keeping in mind that they may be offering to someone not at their location.
2. Have them email, instant message or otherwise get the offer to you.
3. Draw names from a hat, or otherwise randomly match the offers to the participants on the team and announce who has now offered what, to whom. Or, forward the emails on to their respective recipients.
4. A variation: just match names secretly to each other. Challenge the participants to do something nice for the person whose name they got before the next meeting. At the next meeting, report to the team what happened.

FIRST IMPRESSIONS

This is . . . An activity in which participants determine their first impressions of people picked at random from magazines.

The purpose is . . . Participants see how strong and important others' first impression of them can be.

Use this when . . .
- ➤ Individuals interact with customers a great deal.
- ➤ First impressions of the group are critical for their success.
- ➤ Individuals are resisting their uniforms or other aspects of "the look" you want.

Materials you'll need . . .
- ➤ One envelope for each team that contains four or five pictures of people from magazines. Avoid famous or recognizable people. Avoid settings and backgrounds that are not neutral.

Here's how . . .
1. Divide the group into teams of four to six participants.
2. Give each group an envelope containing pictures of various people.
3. They have 6 minutes to discuss their first impressions of the people based solely on what they see in the picture.
4. Have them report back to the larger group on one of the pictures to which their team felt the strongest first impression.

For example . . .	"This woman is probably a professional. Look at the way her head is held up high. She's probably assertive and very sure of herself. Oh, and check out that necklace. Doesn't it just scream "success"? "No, I think that necklace begs for attention! I agree she looks pretty assertive, though. She also seems to. . ."
Ask these questions . . .	➤ How easy was it to agree on your first impressions of these people? ➤ What were some of the reasons for disagreement? *(Different upbringing; Different history with a certain kind of look; etc.)* ➤ What judgments are others making about us and the way we present ourselves? ➤ What implications does this have for us on the job?
Tips for success . . .	➤ Keep the Debrief away from discussing whether first impressions are fair or not. Accept that they happen, and focus on how you can leverage that fact for your organization. ➤ Collect the pictures from various magazines. Try for as eclectic a mix as possible for each envelope. ➤ Be sensitive to racial or gender biases in your group and the pictures. ➤ Give a 1-minute warning before discussions are to end.
Try these variations . . .	➤ You can focus the first impressions specifically just on facial expressions, or clothing, or body language, or whatever else you want to emphasize. ➤ Refocus the Debrief to make this discussion more about diversity—accepting others for who and what they are. After giving out the envelopes of pictures, ask the teams to decide which one they would most want to have join their team, and

which one they would least like to have join their team. Why?

> Have the teams "fix" each picture by identifying how they would improve the look of each one to make them ready to join their team. Focus the Debrief on what they learned from each other concerning how they feel the group should be presenting themselves.

> Ask what product or service each pictured person would be representing or selling.

For virtual teams . . .

This activity works well for virtual teams.

1. Rather than putting pictures in envelopes, scan them and send them to the team members.
2. At Step 3, have the smaller teams meet together elsewhere online or using a separate conference call.
3. At Step 4, reconvene and have the teams post or send the picture they wish to share.
4. Steps 1–3 can be conducted in advance. In the meeting, have teams report out (Step 4) and discuss through the Debrief.

JUNK TO JEWELS

This is . . .	An activity in which participants take work-related items and show how those reflect what each participant brings to the strength of the team.
The purpose is . . .	Participants appreciate their own and each others' contribution to the team's success.
Use this when . . .	➤ A significant project or work effort is beginning. ➤ Individuals are not feeling confident about their ability to get the job done. ➤ Individuals need to bond together.
Materials you'll need . . .	➤ An array of items commonly found in your work environment—paper clips, pens, erasers, calculators, coffee mugs, staplers, sticky notes, rubber bands, and so forth.
Here's how . . .	1. Have each participant select an item that best represents what he or she feels he or she has to contribute to the team's success. 2. Have each participant share with the group why she chose the object she did. 3. Give the team 5 minutes to now make a sculpture using their items. The final sculpture should show how the individual parts would come together to strengthen the team and ensure success.

For example . . .	"I chose a calculator because I tend to be very analytical. I like to find solutions. I get more from the search for the answer than I do from the glory of having found it." "I also chose the calculator, but for me, it is because I am very detail focused. Approximations and guesses are not good enough for me. So I will attend to the details for this group."
Ask these questions . . .	➤ Why is it that the same item meant different things to different people? ➤ What were you thinking as you tried to incorporate everything into a sculpture? *(I wasn't sure how the stapler could be included; I wanted the pen to be more central; Some were more concerned about the finished product than others; etc.)* ➤ What implications does this have for us back on the job?
Tips for success . . .	➤ If the group is large (more than 15 people), divide the group into teams that represent intact work groups. ➤ Have more than one of each item on the table so several participants can choose the same thing (for different reasons?). ➤ A formal Debrief may be unnecessary if you discuss briefly after each participant shares his or her strength.
Try these variations . . .	➤ You can make this activity more personal by having the participants select the item that best reflects their personality, and then explain why. ➤ Make this a development activity. Have the participants select the item that best represents what they want to develop in themselves. Invite the others to support and assist them.

➤ After participants select their items, have the team try to guess why each participant chose what they did.

For virtual teams . . . This activity is not suitable for virtual teams.

KUDOS

This is . . .   A recognition activity in which their peers, not their boss, appreciate the participants.

The purpose is . . .   Participants receive recognition and appreciation from each other and have it reinforced by the whole team.

Use this when . . .
- ➤ A significant project or work effort has been completed—to celebrate the success.
- ➤ Individuals are feeling down or less confident about themselves.
- ➤ Individuals need to recognize and appreciate what's going right among themselves.
- ➤ Individuals need to bond together.

Materials you'll need . . .
- ➤ A box or two of Kudos® candy bars.

Here's how . . .
1. Show a box of Kudos® bars to the group, and make sure everyone knows what the word kudos means.
2. Explain that they are to use the candy bars to recognize each other for things they have accomplished.
3. Anyone can give anyone else a candy bar. They can give more than one, if they like.
4. The only stipulation is that it must be accompanied by a brief, but *specific* explanation of why.
5. Do not go in any order. Do not require anyone to give a candy bar. Let this be entirely voluntary.

6. You go first. Give a Kudos® bar to a participant. As you do, explain what that person did to receive the bar.

7. Encourage the participants to follow your lead—someone (anyone) can now give a candy bar to someone else.

8. Initiate a short round of applause for the recipient after each award.

9. Continue until the enthusiasm dies down, or until you run out of candy bars.

For example . . . "Kudos to Vanessa for helping me research that billing error last Thursday. She helped me whittle down the possible causes for the error. I was able to get back to the customer with an answer much quicker than if I had worked on it by myself."

Ask these questions . . .
➤ How difficult (or easy) was it to give each other recognition? Why?
➤ How does recognition from your peers differ from recognition you get from me?
➤ What do you think would happen if we gave feedback like this to colleagues outside our group (vendors, internal clients, suppliers, customers, support staff, etc.)?

Tips for success . . .
➤ The first participant to give a candy bar may be tentative, but once the concept catches on, participants often start fighting over who gets to recognize whom next (and isn't that a wonderful "fight" to have?).
➤ The recipient of the candy bar is never expected to give one to someone else. Let whoever wants to give a candy bar give one. Do not worry about taking turns or going in order.

- ➤ You may want to tell one participant about the activity beforehand and ask him to be prepared to hand out a candy bar after you do, just to get the ball rolling.
- ➤ You can use this as a regular feature of your on-going staff meetings. It never gets old, and the participants will never run out of things to recognize and appreciate in each other.
- ➤ Keep the recognition on par with the reward. If someone does something truly outstanding, perhaps something more than a candy bar is appropriate.
- ➤ Don't worry about everyone getting a candy bar. This is not about fairness. (Maybe those who do not get one this time will think about why they did not get recognized, and change.) This is especially okay if you make this activity a regular or semiregular activity for the group.
- ➤ If someone gives a candy bar and is not specific, ask them to share an example (not to "test" them, but to give the rest of the group an idea of what specifically is being recognized).

Try these variations . . .
- ➤ You can use other small rewards besides Kudos® bars—perhaps something more relevant to your organization.
- ➤ Give a candy bar to each participant, and have each give it to someone else in recognition or appreciation.

For Virtual teams . . .
This activity works well for virtual teams.
1. Do the activity without the candy bars. Start by explaining the rules of the activity without the use of candy bars. Be the first to recognize someone. Be specific. Then open it up for anyone to recognize anyone else.

2. Or, have the group use virtual candy bars. When the activity is over, send candy bars to anyone who was given one by their teammate.
3. If most of the team are at one location, do the activity as described and have someone act as proxy for the few who are connected via phone or video. Later mail the candy bars to them.
4. Each variation listed can work for a virtual team using one of the alternatives above.

LABELS

This is . . .   A planning activity in which participants treat each other differently based on written labels they wear on their foreheads.

The purpose is . . .   Participants learn first hand how it feels to be treated a certain way because of generalizations or prejudices. They learn how this hampers good communication.

Use this when . . .
- ➤ The group needs to appreciate the diversity of its members better.
- ➤ Individuals are approaching each other, customers, partners, or others with preconceived notions about them.
- ➤ Labels and prejudices are getting in the way of communication and collaboration.

Materials you'll need . . .
- ➤ A set of six labels for each group. Labels should be large enough that participants can read them from several feet away.
- ➤ Labels can be directive, like "disagree with me," "ignore me," "treat me like the leader," "laugh at me," "respect my opinions," "find fault with me," "argue with me," "agree with me," "interrupt me," and so forth. Or, they can be simple labels, such as "arrogant," "helpful," "self-promoting," "brown-noser," "cooperative," "a pushover," "defensive," "leader," and so forth.

1. Divide the group into teams of six participants.
2. Distribute a set of six labels to each team, face down.
3. Each team member sticks a label on the forehead of the person next to him or her.
4. All participants can read what is on others' labels but not their own. Do not tell anyone what is on his or her own label.
5. Give the teams a task to plan (plan a departmental picnic, how they will participate in this year's community fund raiser, etc.). They will have 7 minutes to do this.
6. As they discuss, they must respect the label each participant is wearing. React and respond according to what it says.
7. After 7 minutes, even if the task is not complete, stop the teams and discuss.

**Ask these
questions . . .**

➤ What happened? Did you accomplish your task? Why or why not?

➤ How satisfied are you with the outcome? Why?

➤ How did you feel about treating people with these labels? *(It was not me; It felt forced; It was fun; etc.)* Did it get easier over time? Why? *(Others reinforced the label; I got used to treating her that way; etc.)*

➤ How did you feel about the way you were being treated? *(Frustrated; angry; puzzled; annoyed; etc.)* What was your reaction then? *(I fought harder; I disengaged; I treated him even worse; etc.)*

➤ What implications does this have for us back on the job?

**Tips for
success . . .**

➤ Use your judgment in dividing teams. For example, if you have 11 participants, remove one label from one set, and have one team of 6 and one team of

5 participants, so that everyone can have the experience. If there are 13 participants, have a seventh label ready.

➤ Some people may be reluctant to adhere to the labels. As you observe, encourage participants to take the labels they see to heart and act accordingly.

Try these variations . . .

➤ Try different labels or different combinations of labels with different teams to explore various themes or dynamics.

➤ Precede this activity with an activity to reinforce creativity and individuality. Have each participant make a paper hat from newsprint. Then affix the labels to the participants' hats and have them wear them for this activity.

➤ Make the labels represent different stakeholders on a project or different types of customers and so forth.

➤ Have only one group of six to eight participants with labels do the task, while the rest of your group observes. The Debrief can be directed to the participants and then the observers.

➤ Use only a few labels for only a few people in the group.

➤ Instead of planning a picnic, have the teams grapple with a real work-related problem or issue.

For virtual teams . . .

This activity is not suitable for virtual teams.

THANK-YOU CARDS

This is . . .   A recognition activity in which team members appreciate each other's contributions to the team, a project, or some other significant work effort.

The purpose is . . .   Participants give and receive appreciation for individual and group efforts.

Use this when . . .

➤ The successful completion of a significant project or work effort should be celebrated.

➤ Individuals need to recognize and appreciate what's going well among themselves.

➤ Periodically, to have the team continually reinforce their collective and individual contributions.

Materials you'll need . . .

➤ One or more decks of playing cards—all number cards removed.

Here's how . . .

1. Shuffle the face cards (including aces) and deal them out, one to each participant.
2. Take turns sharing a story of appreciation based on the following code:
    ➤ Jack: an individual team member.
    ➤ Queen: the team as a whole.
    ➤ King: yourself.
    ➤ Ace: the team's leader.

3. Initiate a short round of applause after each "thank you."

For example . . .
"Thank you Patti for taking me under your wing and showing me the ropes. You really helped me come up to speed quickly when you. . . ."

"Thank you team for coming together when we most needed to last week. I was afraid we were going to lose the deal until. . . ."

"I thank myself for having the courage to ask that question early on about how this project would impact our colleagues in Ireland and Japan. I was afraid to bring that up, but. . . ."

"Thank you Ms. Boss for trusting me when the city rejected our permit request and I wanted you to fix the problem for me. Instead you. . . ."

Ask these questions . . .
➤ How difficult (or easy) was it to give each other thanks?
➤ To whom was it easiest (or most difficult) to give thanks? Why?
➤ How did you feel giving yourself recognition in front of the team? *(I felt awkward; I felt self-serving; I didn't think I should be calling myself out; I wanted to say more but didn't want to come across as arrogant; etc.).*
➤ Who, outside of our team, should we also recognize and thank?

Tips for success . . .
➤ After dealing the cards and explaining the game, give people 1 to 2 minutes to quietly think about what they are going to say.
➤ Use a second deck if the group is larger than 15.
➤ If someone gives feedback and is not very specific ("She was so helpful!") ask them to share an example ("Great! Will you share an example of one

of the ways she was helpful?"). This is not to test them, but to give the group (and her!) a better sense of why she is being thanked and recognized.

Try these variations . . .	➤ Give each participant a set of all 4 cards. Allow several minutes for them to gather their thoughts. Then have them take turns sharing a "thank you" for one card at a time.
	➤ Make the activity more impromptu by not dealing the cards. Shuffle and then place the deck face down. Participants take turns drawing a card and then expressing thanks.
	➤ Use the "thank yous" throughout a long meeting. After dealing the cards and explaining the game, conduct the meeting as usual. Except, periodically, take a "thank you break" and call on another participant to share their recognition.

For virtual teams . . .	This activity works well for virtual teams.
	1. Have a deck of cards available at each location.
	2. Then follow Steps 2 to 3.
	3. Most of the variations listed can work for a virtual team.

WHAT I LIKE ABOUT ME

This is . . . A discussion activity in which participants tell each other what their own strengths are.

The purpose is . . . Participants realize how much they have to offer, how valuable they are to the team, and that it's okay to acknowledge their own accomplishments.

Use this when . . .
- ➤ Individuals need a boost of self-esteem.
- ➤ Individuals are not feeling confident about their ability to get the job done.
- ➤ You don't have prep time and/or materials for anything more elaborate.

Materials you'll need . . .
- ➤ No materials are necessary for this activity.

Here's how . . .
1. Have the participants pair up.
2. One partner will talk to the other one for 3 minutes nonstop about what they have accomplished at work lately.
3. If the speaker says anything that diminishes or minimizes their accomplishment, the listener will say, "I object." The speaker must then retract their comment.
4. Other than that, the listener may not speak at all.
5. After 3 minutes, reverse roles and repeat.

For example . . .	Speaker: "I did a good job on the XYZ account. When they called and asked me those tough questions, at first I was baffled. Then I asked Michael for help, and I felt more comfortable answering them. Of course, Michael probably could have handled it better without me, but at least I was able to. . ." Listener: "I object!" Speaker: "OK, scratch that. I was able to answer their questions with Michael's help. Period. Let's see, another thing I did was. . ."
Ask these questions . . .	➤ Which role was easier for you, the listener or the speaker? Why? *(Most will say the listener.)* ➤ How did you feel about listening without being able to ask questions or contribute your own thoughts? *(Stifled; not part of the conversation; not sure I was understanding; bored; etc.)* ➤ How did you feel about speaking without being able to check in with your listener? *(Egotistical; not sure she was "with" me; unsure of myself; etc.)* ➤ What did you learn about how you feel about yourself? *(I need validation; I'm not comfortable acknowledging my own strengths; I put too much [or too little] emphasis on what others think of me; etc.)* ➤ How do you think this affects how you do your job?
Tips for success . . .	➤ The hardest thing for the speakers will be talking continuously. They may hesitate to acknowledge their contributions. This may come out as they pause to "think of something good." Encourage the speakers to just keep talking. If they run out of things to talk about, tell them to go back in time and keep going back, even if they end up talking about things they did 15 years ago. The point is to realize and acknowledge their own

value and contributions without editing or censoring.

Try these variations . . .

➤ Add competitiveness. The listener gets 1 point every time the speaker pauses for more than 5 seconds and 5 points every time the listener catches them with an "I object." Be prepared with small prizes for the winner. Ask later if the competitive pressure impacted the speaker.

➤ Limit the speakers' monologues to a specific project they have worked on recently as a team. This will help them highlight the diverse and important contributions each has made to the success of the team.

➤ Limit the speakers' monologues to a specific organizational value or core competency. This will help them reinforce those appropriate behaviors in themselves and in each other.

➤ Have the participants answer the discussion questions in their pairs, rather than in the larger group.

For virtual teams . . .

This activity works well for virtual teams. If audio is not available, participants may type in their comments. Each of the variations listed can work for a virtual team.

INDEX

ABOUT THE AUTHOR

Brian Cole Miller is the founder of Working Solutions (Columbus, Ohio), which specializes in building more confident and competent Front Line Leaders (www.WorkingSolutionsOnline.com). He has provided training, coaching, and consulting to clients that include Nationwide Insurance, Franklin Covey, Anthem Blue Cross Blue Shield, and UPS.